AESTHETIC BRIDGES

INDIAN THEORY MEETS AFRICAN NARRATIVES

DR. R. MALATHI, MS. PREETHY C N

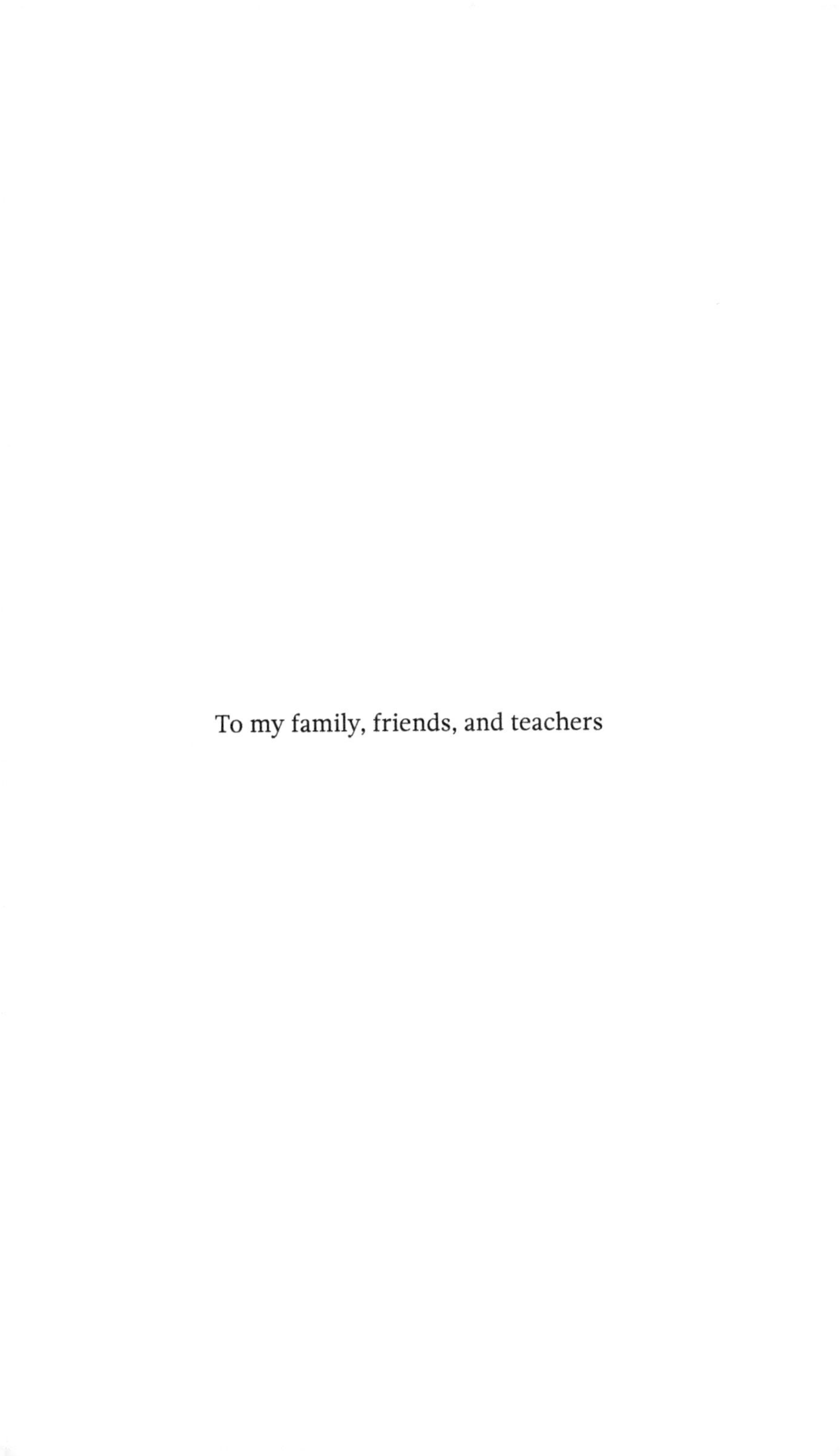

To my family, friends, and teachers

Contents

Epigraph

You are what your deep, driving desire is.
As your desire is, so is your will.
As your will is, so is your deed.
As your deed is, so is your destiny.
— Brihadāranyaka Upanishad

Acknowledgements

The journey of bringing this book to life has been both challenging and deeply rewarding, and it would not have been possible without the invaluable support of numerous individuals and institutions.I am profoundly grateful to the Almighty for granting me the strength, perseverance, and clarity needed to bring this work to fruition. Through divine guidance and blessings, I have been able to undertake and complete this journey, and I remain deeply humbled by this support.

I am deeply grateful to my supervisor and mentor, **Dr. R. Malathi** whose unwavering guidance and insightful feedback have been instrumental throughout this process. Her expertise and dedication to fostering intellectual growth have shaped my understanding and strengthened this work. My heartfelt thanks to my colleagues and fellow researchers in the Department of English at Nehru Arts and Science College, Thirumalayampalayam, Coimbatore, for their camaraderie, encouragement, and intellectual exchange.

Additionally, I am thankful for the support of my family, whose patience and encouragement provided me with strength during the most demanding times.

Finally, this book is a tribute to the rich cultural heritage of Indian and African literary traditions. I hope that it will contribute to the ongoing dialogue between these two vibrant cultures and inspire future scholars to explore further intersections between aesthetics and narratives.

Thank you all for making this endeavor possible.
Preethy C N

Preface

The worlds of Indian and African literature are vast, rich, and steeped in histories that span millennia. Deep-rooted cultural practices, languages, philosophies, and artistic traditions shape them. At first glance, the geographical distance and historical specificity of Indian and African cultures might seem to set them on divergent paths. However, a closer examination reveals shared human experiences and cultural dynamics that transcend borders—experiences that speak of identity, power, love, suffering, and the resilience of the human spirit.

This book, *Aesthetic Bridges: Indian Theory Meets African Narratives*, seeks to create a cross-cultural dialogue by applying the principles of Indian aesthetics to African postcolonial narratives. Indian poetics, with its profound concepts of *Dhvani* (suggestion), *Rasa* (emotion or aesthetic flavor), and *Alankāra* (figurative speech), provides a nuanced lens through which literature can be read and understood. Meanwhile, African narratives—rooted in oral traditions, colonial histories, and postcolonial realities—offer powerful stories of survival, identity, and resistance. By bringing these two traditions into conversation, this book aims to enrich our understanding of both, allowing new insights to emerge through their interaction.

Indian aesthetic theory, as elaborated by thinkers like Bharata, Ānandavardhana, and Abhinavagupta, offers a sophisticated way of understanding how literature evokes emotions and meanings, often beyond the literal. These aesthetic principles, while born in the classical Sanskrit tradition, are not confined to Indian literature. They are, in fact, versatile tools that can illuminate texts from different cultures and epochs. African literature, with its profound engagement with themes of colonization, gender, identity, and community, provides fertile ground for such exploration. The application of Indian poetics to these narratives helps uncover latent emotional resonances and hidden power dynamics that might otherwise go unnoticed.

This book draws upon postcolonial African texts by authors such as Buchi Emecheta and Chimamanda Ngozi Adichie. These works, steeped in the historical and cultural contexts of postcolonial Africa, explore the intricacies of gender, power, identity, and survival. In examining them through the lens of Indian aesthetics, I explore how *Dhvani* (suggestion) and *Rasa* (aesthetic flavor) enhance our understanding of the characters' emotional landscapes, the cultural silences, and the nuanced forms of resistance and empowerment present in these texts.

In addition to these critical explorations, this work also serves as a celebration of the universality of human emotion and artistic expression. Both Indian and African traditions emphasize storytelling as central to their cultures—whether through the poetic theories of Indian thinkers or the oral traditions of African griots and storytellers. By examining these traditions in tandem, this book highlights the global resonance of literary forms and emotional expressions, demonstrating that art and literature have the capacity to transcend cultural boundaries and create bridges of understanding.

At its core, *Aesthetic Bridges* is an invitation to readers to explore the intersection of Indian and African literary traditions, not merely as an intellectual exercise but as a journey of aesthetic appreciation. It is a reminder that, while the cultural specifics of these traditions may differ, their emotional truths and artistic visions speak to a shared human experience. This convergence, I believe, offers us a richer understanding of literature and a deeper appreciation of the diverse yet interconnected ways in which humanity expresses itself through art.

I would like to express my deep gratitude to those who have supported me in this endeavor. My mentors and colleagues have provided invaluable guidance and encouragement throughout this project. I am especially indebted to my family, whose unwavering support has been my greatest source of strength. Finally, I owe a debt of gratitude to the rich literary traditions of both India and Africa, whose timeless beauty and wisdom continue to inspire and challenge scholars and readers alike.

With this book, I hope to contribute to the global conversation on literature, aesthetics, and the shared power of storytelling. May this work serve as a humble bridge between cultures, and may it inspire further exploration into the connections between diverse literary traditions and their interpretations.

INTRODUCTION

The intersections of different aesthetic traditions offer fertile ground for new understandings and creative dialogues in a world rich with diverse cultures and artistic expressions. *Aesthetic Bridges: Indian Theory Meets African Narratives* embarks on a journey across continents, bringing together the philosophical underpinnings of Indian aesthetics with the vibrant storytelling traditions of Africa. This book seeks to illuminate the common threads and distinct nuances that arise when these two cultural forces meet.

Indian and African Cultures: A Brief Overview

Indian and African cultures, though geographically distant, share a commonality in the depth, diversity, and richness of their oral and literary traditions. Indian culture, with its roots in ancient Vedic traditions, is marked by a deep reverence for spirituality, philosophy, and the arts. The Indian subcontinent has given rise to a wide array of artistic expressions, from classical music and dance to intricate visual arts and elaborate literary traditions. The concept of aesthetic experience, is central to Indian art and literature, providing a framework for understanding the emotional and spiritual impact of artistic expression.

African culture, on the other hand, is a tapestry woven from the diverse traditions of its numerous ethnic groups and societies. African narratives are deeply embedded in the oral tradition, where storytelling, music, dance, and performance play a crucial role in the transmission of knowledge, values, and history. The continent's artistic expressions are varied, encompassing everything from the intricate beadwork of the Maasai to the rhythm and movement of West African drumming and dance. Despite the differences in form and medium, African art and narratives often serve similar functions to those in Indian culture—preserving history, conveying moral lessons, and expressing the complexities of the human experience.

Though separated by geography, India and Africa share histories marked by colonialism, spirituality, and a profound respect for oral and written traditions. Indian aesthetic theories, deeply rooted in ancient texts like the *Nātyaṣāstra* and enriched by centuries of philosophical discourse, provide a framework for understanding the essence of art, beauty, and emotional expression. On the other hand, African narratives, with their rich oral traditions, folklore, and contemporary literature, offer a dynamic canvas where these aesthetic principles can be explored, challenged, and expanded.

Indian aesthetics is a rich and intricate field that reflects the cultural, philosophical, and spiritual heritage of India. It encompasses various forms of art, including visual arts, music, dance, literature, and theatre. Indian aesthetics is deeply rooted in the country's history, religion, and philosophy, offering a unique perspective on beauty, expression, and the purpose of art. This work delves into how Indian theories of rasa (aesthetic emotion), Dhvani (suggestion), and Alamkāra (ornamentation), Vakrokthi, Guna, and Rīti resonate within African stories, myths, and literary forms. By examining this cross-cultural dialogue, *Aesthetic Bridges: Indian Theory Meets African Narratives* seeks to uncover new layers of meaning in both traditions, offering readers a deeper appreciation of the universal and the particular in human creativity.

As we navigate through these aesthetic encounters, the book also addresses broader questions: How do different cultures perceive beauty and art? What happens when two distinct artistic traditions interact? Can the meeting of Indian and African aesthetics lead to new forms of expression? Through these questions, this book serves as a scholarly exploration and an invitation to celebrate the richness of global cultural exchanges.

African Narratives: Oral Tradition and Storytelling

African narratives are predominantly rooted in the oral tradition, where storytelling is a communal activity that serves multiple purposes—educational, entertainment, spiritual, and social. African oral literature is rich with proverbs, myths, folktales, and epics that have been passed down through generations. These stories often serve as vehicles for conveying cultural values, moral lessons, and collective memory.

Unlike the more formalized structures of written literature, African oral narratives are characterized by their fluidity and adaptability. Storytellers, or "griots", play a crucial role in this tradition, using their skills to engage audiences, preserve history, and address contemporary issues. The performative aspect of African storytelling—where music, dance, and visual art often accompany the spoken word—adds layers of meaning and enhances the emotional impact of the narratives.

Bridging the Gap: Indian Theory and African Narratives

The intersection of Indian aesthetic theory and African narratives offers a fertile ground for cross-cultural exploration and understanding. While the Indian concept of Rasa provides a structured framework for analyzing the emotional impact of art, African narratives offer a rich tapestry of stories that are deeply rooted in communal experience and oral tradition. By applying Rasa theory to African narratives, we can gain new insights into the ways these stories evoke emotion and convey meaning.

Conversely, the dynamism and performative nature of African storytelling can enrich our understanding of Indian aesthetic theory, particularly in its application to contemporary and oral forms of expression. The fusion of these two traditions allows for a more holistic approach to the study of aesthetics, one that transcends cultural boundaries and highlights the universal power of narrative.

Chapter Overviews

As we journey through this exploration of Indian aesthetic theory and African narratives, the following chapters will delve deeper into specific themes and concepts that underscore the aesthetic connections between these two traditions:

Foundation of Aesthetic Thought:

This chapter lays the groundwork for understanding the core principles of aesthetic theory in both Indian and African contexts. We will explore the philosophical underpinnings of Indian aesthetics, focusing on the *Nātyashāstra* and its influence on art, literature, and performance. In parallel, we will examine African aesthetic thought as it manifests in various cultural practices, from storytelling to visual arts. The chapter aims to establish a comparative framework highlighting the shared emphasis on beauty, emotion, and the human experience in both traditions.

Emotional Landscapes:

Building on the foundation of aesthetic thought, this chapter delves into the emotional dimensions of Indian and African narratives. Rasa's categorization of emotions, will be applied to African stories, exploring how these narratives evoke feelings of love, heroism, fear, and more. We will also consider how African concepts of emotion and feeling intersect with Indian aesthetic theory, offering new perspectives on the emotional landscapes within these cultural expressions.

Performance and Participation:

Performance is a central aspect of both Indian and African cultures, where art is often experienced in communal settings. This chapter examines the role of performance in both traditions, from Indian classical dance and theater to African music and dance rituals. We will explore how participation in these performances—whether as performers or audience members—enhances the aesthetic experience and deepens the connection to the cultural and emotional content of the narratives.

Symbolism and Spirituality:

The final chapter focuses on the rich symbolism and spiritual dimensions present in Indian and African narratives. Symbolism in Indian art often carries deep spiritual significance, connecting the material world with the divine. Similarly, African narratives are replete with symbols that convey spiritual and moral messages. By examining these symbolic elements, we will uncover how both traditions use art to explore and express spiritual truths, offering a window into the metaphysical aspects of human existence.

This introductory chapter has set the stage for a deeper exploration of the connections between Indian aesthetic theory and African narratives. By examining the cultural foundations and narrative traditions of these two regions, we can begin to appreciate how they complement and inform each other. Through this cross-cultural dialogue, we hope to build bridges between these two rich traditions, fostering a greater understanding of the universal themes that unite them.

Post-Colonial Narratives:

This chapter addresses the impact of colonialism on Indian and African cultural expressions and the subsequent emergence of post-colonial narratives that seek to reclaim, redefine, and reassert cultural identities. We will explore how Indian and African writers, artists, and performers have used aesthetic traditions to challenge colonial legacies, resist cultural imperialism, and articulate new visions of identity and belonging. By analyzing post-colonial literature, film, and performance, we will see how these narratives provide a powerful critique of historical injustices while simultaneously celebrating the resilience and creativity of Indian and African cultures. This chapter will highlight how post-colonial narratives utilize the frameworks of Rasa theory and African oral traditions to forge new aesthetic expressions rooted in cultural pride and self-determination.

This introductory chapter has set the stage for a deeper exploration of the connections between Indian aesthetic theory and African narratives. By examining the cultural foundations and narrative traditions of these two regions, we can begin to appreciate how they complement and inform each other. In the chapters that follow, we will delve into specific themes, applying the principles of Rasa theory to uncover new dimensions of meaning and emotional resonance in African narratives. Through this cross-cultural dialogue, we hope to build bridges between these two rich traditions, fostering a greater understanding of the universal themes that unite them.

CHAPTER TWO

FOUNDATION OF AESTHETIC THOUGHT

The foundation of aesthetic thought in Indian culture is a rich tapestry woven from various schools of thought that have developed over centuries. Indian aesthetics is deeply intertwined with spiritual, philosophical, and literary traditions, offering profound insights into the nature of beauty, emotion, and artistic expression. This chapter will delve into the history of Indian aesthetics and explore key concepts such as *Rasa*, *Dhvani*, *Guna*, *Riti*, *Vakrokti*, and *Alamkara* schools of thought. By examining these concepts, we can understand how Indian aesthetic theory provides a nuanced framework for interpreting art, literature, and performance.

The Historical Context of Indian Aesthetics

Indian poetics, or *Sāhitya Śāstra*, has a long and intricate history that stretches back thousands of years, rooted in the rich philosophical, linguistic, and cultural traditions of India. The development of these schools of thought reflects not just literary criticism but a deep engagement with aesthetics, linguistics, and psychology. The diverse schools of Indian poetics reflect varying interpretations of what constitutes literature, what its primary functions are, and how best it can be appreciated.

The foundations of Indian poetics can be traced to ancient texts like the *Vedas*, where poetic language was already seen as a powerful force in expressing cosmic truths. The hymns of the *Rigveda*, composed between 1500 and 1200 BCE, are rich with metaphors, symbolism, and a deep understanding of rhythm and meter. These early compositions focused on conveying religious and philosophical ideas, but they also highlight a nascent awareness of literary techniques that would later be formalized. In the Vedic tradition, language itself was seen as sacred, and the proper articulation of words was believed to have both spiritual and material consequences. This reverence for language laid the groundwork for later aesthetic theories that would explore the emotive and suggestive power of words.

As the Vedic tradition evolved, the epics *Mahābhārata* and *Rāmāyaṇa* became central to Indian culture, shaping both the literary imagination and the development of literary theory. These epics, composed between 500 BCE and 200 CE, are not only monumental literary achievements but also represent an early stage in the conscious use of narrative structure, emotional resonance, and poetic technique. The *Mahābhārata*, for instance, is known for its intricate narratives that weave together philosophical discourse with powerful emotional experiences. The characters' inner lives and their emotional journeys provided a fertile ground for later theories like *Rasa* to explore how literature can evoke specific emotions in its audience.

Indian aesthetic theory has its roots in ancient texts and has evolved through various philosophical discourses over millennia. The earliest references to aesthetic thought can be traced back to the *Vedas* and *Upanishads*, where art, music, and poetry were seen as expressions of the divine. The development of formal aesthetic theory, however, is attributed to texts like the *Natya Shastra* by Bharata Muni, which dates back to between 200 BCE and 200 CE. This comprehensive treatise on drama, dance, and music laid the foundation for the Rasa theory and became the cornerstone of Indian aesthetics.

Over the centuries, various scholars and poets contributed to the evolution of Indian aesthetic thought. Key figures include Abhinavagupta, who provided a detailed commentary on *Natya Shastra* and expanded on the concept of Rasa, Anandavardhana, who introduced the Dhvani theory, and Kuntaka, who developed the Vakrokti school. Each of these scholars brought unique perspectives that enriched the understanding of art and aesthetics in the Indian context.

Key Concepts in Indian Aesthetic Theory

1. The Concept of Rasa

The concept of *Rasa* is central to Indian aesthetics and refers to the emotional essence or flavor evoked by a work of art. Bharata Muni's *Natyashāstra* defines Rasa as the outcome of a harmonious combination of various emotional states (*bhavas*) expressed through artistic performance, ultimately leading to a transformative experience for the audience. *Rasa* refers to the distilled emotion or flavor that a work of art evokes in the viewer or reader. Bharatamuni identified eight primary *Rasas*—love, humor, sorrow, anger, heroism, fear, disgust, and wonder—and these became the cornerstones of Indian aesthetic theory.

Bharatamuni's *Rasa* theory suggests that the ultimate goal of literature, especially poetry and drama, is to evoke a specific emotion in the audience, which leads to a cathartic or transformative experience. Each *Rasa* corresponds to a particular emotion (*bhāva*) that the characters in a play or poem experience, and through careful crafting of the narrative and linguistic elements, the audience can also experience these emotions in a heightened, purified form. This aesthetic response, according to Bharatamuni, leads to a deeper understanding of the human condition and the ultimate experience of transcendence, especially in the case of *Śānta Rasa*, the ninth *Rasa* that was later added to the original eight by theorists such as Abhinavagupta. *Śānta Rasa* focuses on tranquility or spiritual peace, reflecting the deep connection between aesthetics and metaphysics in Indian thought.

The famous aphorism from *Natyashastra* states:

"Vibhavanubhava Vyabhichari Samyogad Rasa Nishpattih" (*Natya Shastra*, Chapter 6, Verse 31), which means that Rasa arises from the combination of determinants (*Vibhāvās*), consequents (*Anubhāvās*), and transitory emotional states (*Vyabhichāri bhavas*).

The *Nātyashāstra* outlines nine primary Rasas, known as *Nava Rasa*:

1. Srigara (Love/Beauty)
2. Hasya (Laughter/Comedy)
3. Karuna (Compassion/Sorrow)
4. Raudra (Anger)
5. Veera (Heroism)
6. Bhayānaka (Fear)
7. Bībhatsa (Disgust)
8. Adbhuta (Wonder)
9. Shanta (Peace/Tranquility)

Each Rasa is associated with specific colors, deities, and emotions, making it a holistic framework that integrates aesthetic, psychological, and spiritual dimensions. The ultimate goal of Rasa is to elevate both the artist and the audience to a higher state of emotional and spiritual realization, known as *Rasānanda*. The *Rasa* theory was later developed and refined by various scholars, most notably Abhinavagupta in the 10th century. Abhinavagupta, a Kashmiri philosopher and aesthetician, elaborated on the *Nātyaśāstra* and provided his own interpretations of *Rasa* in his works like the *Abhinavabhāratī*. He emphasized the concept of *sādhāranīkarana*, the process of universalization, where individual emotions are abstracted in such a way that they can be universally experienced by the audience. For Abhinavagupta, *Rasa* is not merely an emotional response but a spiritual one, leading to a profound sense of self-awareness and unity with the cosmos. His interpretation of

Rasa as a vehicle for spiritual insight was deeply influenced by the non-dualistic Shaiva philosophy of Kashmir, which sees the universe and individual consciousness as interconnected.

2. The Concept of Dhvani

The *Dhvani* theory, introduced by Anandavardhana in his work *Dhvanyaloka* (Light on Dhvani), emphasizes the power of suggestion in poetry and literature. *Dhvani,* literally meaning "sound" or "echo", refers to the implied meaning or suggestive power that transcends the literal and conventional meanings of words. Anandavardhana argued that the essence of poetry lies not in its direct expression but in what it suggests beyond the obvious. He states: "Dhvani is that in which the meaning is suggested through words, surpassing their primary or secondary meanings" (*Dhvanyaloka*, p. 23).

Dhvani theory focuses on three levels of meaning:

1. Abhidha (literal meaning)
2. Lakshana (indicative meaning)
3. Vyanjana (suggestive meaning)

It is the *Vyanjana,* or the suggestive meaning, that evokes Rasa and provides the reader or listener with a deeper aesthetic experience. This theory has had a profound influence on the understanding of poetic language and its capacity to convey complex emotions and ideas.

3. The Concept of Guna

The concept of *Guna* refers to the qualities or attributes that contribute to the aesthetic excellence of a work of art. Traditionally, ten Gunas have been identified, which are considered essential for creating artistic beauty and elegance. These qualities include:

1. Ojas (vigor or vitality)
2. Prasada (clarity)
3. Saukumarya (softness or delicacy)
4. Samata (equanimity or balance)
5. Madhurya (sweetness)
6. Arthavyakti (clarity of meaning)
7. Udarata (grandeur)
8. Saukshmya (subtlety)
9. Kanti (brilliance)
10. Samadhi (coherence)

These Gunas help in determining the stylistic elegance and effectiveness of artistic expression. By adhering to these qualities, poets and artists can create works that are aesthetically pleasing and capable of evoking profound emotional responses.

4. The Concept of Riti

Riti refers to the style or mode of expression used in literature and art. According to the *Riti* school of thought, aesthetic excellence is achieved through the proper use of language and poetic devices. Different *Ritis* are associated with different emotions and themes, and they play a crucial role in shaping the overall aesthetic experience.

The primary *Ritis* identified in Indian aesthetics are:

1. Vaidarbhi Riti: Characterized by softness, simplicity, and elegance, often used in conveying love and tenderness.
2. Gaudiya Riti: Marked by complexity, grandeur, and elaboration, suitable for heroic and lofty themes.
3. Panchali Riti: A blend of Vaidarbhi and Gaudiya styles, known for its balanced and versatile expression.

The concept of *Riti* highlights the importance of style and diction in achieving the desired aesthetic impact, making it a critical aspect of poetic and artistic creation. In contrast to the *Alamkāra* school, the *Rīti* or style school of Indian poetics focused on the way language is used to create a particular stylistic effect. The *Rīti* school became prominent with the work of Vāmana, an 8th-century scholar who defined *Rīti* as the soul of poetry. For Vāmana, poetry's effectiveness lay in its choice of words, their arrangement, and the overall style of expression. The *Rīti* school thus contributed to the understanding of how style shapes the reader's experience and how it can be used to reflect the content of the poem in a harmonious way.

5. The Concept of Vakrokthi

The *Vakrokthi* school, developed by Kuntaka, emphasizes the importance of oblique or indirect expression in art and literature. *Vakrokthi* means "crooked speech" or "deviation," suggesting that the beauty of language lies in its ability to convey meaning in a nuanced and figurative manner. Kuntaka defines *Vakrokthi* as: "The special mode of speech that makes the ordinary language extraordinary by its deviations and twists" (Kuntaka, *Vakroktijivita*, p. 41).

According to Kuntaka, there are six types of *Vakrokthi*:

1. Varna Vakrokthi (phonetic deviation)
2. Pada Vakrokthi (word deviation)
3. Vākya Vakrokthi (sentence deviation)
4. Prakarana Vakrokthi (contextual deviation)
5. Prabandha Vakrokthi (compositional deviation)
6. Alamkara Vakrokthi (figural deviation)

Vakrokti emphasizes the artistic creativity involved in using language innovatively to evoke emotional and aesthetic responses, thus enriching the overall impact of the literary or artistic work.

6. The Alamkara School

Alongside the *Rasa* theory, other schools of Indian poetics also emerged, each offering its own perspective on the function and nature of literature. The *Alamkāra* school, which focused on figures of speech and ornamentation, is one of the oldest traditions in Indian poetics, with roots going back to the early classical period. The *Alamkara* school of thought, which means "ornamentation" focuses on the use of rhetorical devices and figures of speech to enhance the beauty and impact of poetry and literature. Poets and scholars of this school, such as Bhāmaha in the 6th century and later Udbhaṭa and Rudraṭa, identified a variety of *alamkāras*, or poetic devices, that enhance the aesthetic appeal of a poem. This school of thought believes that the aesthetic appeal of a work is heightened by the use of *Alamkaras*, which include metaphors, similes, hyperbole, personification, and other literary devices.

Bhamaha, one of the earliest proponents of the *Alamkara* school, argued that:

"The beauty of a poem lies in its ornaments, much like a woman's beauty is enhanced by her jewelry" (Bhamaha, *Kavyalankara*, p. 78).

The *Alamkara* school highlights the importance of artistic embellishment in creating a captivating and aesthetically pleasing work, viewing literary devices as essential tools for the poet or artist to convey deeper meanings and emotions. The *Alamkāra* school, however, was not merely interested in decoration for its own sake. For theorists like Bhāmaha, these poetic devices were essential for conveying meaning and emotion in a more nuanced and layered way. A simple statement might not be enough to convey the depth of feeling or the complexity of a situation, but through the use of metaphor or simile, for instance, a poet could evoke a richer response in the reader. The emphasis here was on the power of language to create multi-dimensional meanings, which resonate on both an intellectual and emotional level.

Comparative Insights and Synthesis

The various schools of Indian aesthetic thought, while distinct, are interrelated and contribute to a comprehensive understanding of the nature of beauty, art, and emotion. The Rasa theory focuses on the emotional experience, Dhvani emphasizes the power of suggestion, Guna deals with qualitative attributes, Riti concerns style, Vakrokti highlights creative expression, and Alamkara stresses the role of literary devices.

Together, these concepts offer a multifaceted approach to aesthetics, providing artists and scholars with tools to analyze, create, and appreciate art that resonates on emotional, intellectual, and spiritual levels. The integration of these theories demonstrates the sophistication and depth of Indian aesthetic thought, making it a valuable framework for understanding not only Indian art and literature but also offering insights into global artistic traditions.

The foundation of Indian aesthetic thought is a rich and complex tapestry that draws from a wide range of philosophical, spiritual, and artistic traditions. By exploring key concepts such as Rasa, Dhvani, Guna, Riti, Vakrokthi, and Alamkara, this chapter has highlighted the depth and diversity of Indian aesthetics. These theories provide a profound understanding of how art can evoke emotions, convey deeper meanings, and reflect the values and beliefs of a culture. The study of these foundational concepts not only enhances our appreciation of Indian art and literature but also contributes to the broader discourse on aesthetics, creativity, and the universal quest for beauty.

Each of these schools contributed to a rich and multifaceted understanding of literature in India. Over time, these schools did not remain static; they interacted with one another, sometimes complementing and sometimes challenging each other's ideas. The result was a dynamic and evolving tradition of poetics that continued to develop well into the medieval period and beyond. Indian poetics thus reflects the broader philosophical currents of Indian thought, where language, aesthetics, and emotion are seen as deeply interconnected, and where the ultimate aim of literature is to offer not only pleasure but also insight into the nature of reality and the human experience.

This detailed chapter explores the foundational theories of Indian aesthetics, offering insights into how various concepts contribute to the creation and appreciation of art. Through this exploration, the rich heritage of Indian aesthetic thought is revealed, demonstrating its enduring influence on artistic expression and cultural identity. In conclusion, the historical trajectory of Indian poetics reveals a complex and nuanced understanding of literature, rooted in both linguistic expertise and deep philosophical inquiry. Over millennia, Indian literary theorists have systematically engaged with the nature of poetry, drama, and the emotive and intellectual impact of words. From the early conceptualization of *Rasa* in the *Nāṭyaśāstra* to the intricate discussions of suggestion in *Dhvani*, Indian poetics has consistently focused on the intersection of form, function, and meaning.

The *Rasa* theory, with its emphasis on evoking aesthetic pleasure and emotional responses, became the cornerstone of Indian literary criticism, influencing all subsequent schools of thought. Bharatamuni's work set the stage for an exploration of how art can produce a transformative experience, both emotionally and spiritually, a theme that continued to resonate through the later contributions of Abhinavagupta. His philosophical expansion of *Rasa*, especially the addition of *Śānta* as the ninth emotion, reflects the deep integration of aesthetics and metaphysics within Indian intellectual traditions.

Simultaneously, the *Alamkāra* school contributed to the detailed analysis of literary devices, establishing that figures of speech and rhetorical flourishes are not mere embellishments but essential to enhancing the emotive and cognitive dimensions of poetry. The precise categorization of these devices by Bhāmaha and others underlined the technical sophistication with which Indian scholars approached literary works.

The emergence of the *Rīti* school with Vāmana's focus on style further advanced the discourse, showing that the way language is used—its rhythm, texture, and tone—plays a critical role in shaping a poem's meaning and emotional resonance. Meanwhile, the *Dhvani* school, pioneered by Ānandavardhana, brought the reader's interpretative role to the forefront, suggesting that meaning often lies beyond the literal, in the realm of suggestion. This insight marked a significant development in Indian poetics, as it recognized the dynamic interplay between the poet's intentions and the reader's imaginative engagement.

Kuntaka's *Vakrokti* theory, with its emphasis on oblique expression, added another layer of complexity to the analysis of poetic language. By focusing on how deviation from ordinary speech can create depth and evoke powerful emotions, Kuntaka reinforced the idea that poetry's beauty lies in its capacity to transcend the mundane. Finally, Kṣemendra's *Aucitya* theory brought attention to the importance of appropriateness, arguing that the aesthetic and moral coherence of a literary work depends on the harmonious alignment of all its elements.

Collectively, these schools of thought demonstrate that Indian poetics is not a monolithic or static field, but one marked by continual evolution and dialogue. While each school presents a unique perspective on what makes literature effective, they share a common understanding that poetry is not simply a craft but an art form that engages with the deepest aspects of human emotion, thought, and experience. By carefully analyzing language, structure, and emotion, Indian theorists developed a comprehensive framework that addresses both the technical and philosophical dimensions of literature.

The enduring relevance of Indian poetics is evident not only in its historical influence but also in its continued application to modern literary analysis. As contemporary scholars revisit and reinterpret these classical theories, the timeless insights of Indian poetics continue to inspire new ways of thinking about literature, aesthetics, and the role of art in society. Whether through the lens of *Rasa*, *Dhvani*, or *Aucitya*, Indian poetics offers a profound understanding of how words can move, inspire, and enlighten both the mind and the heart.

In the broader context of global literary traditions, Indian poetics stands out for its unique integration of emotional, intellectual, and spiritual dimensions. The focus on the audience's emotional experience, the nuanced use of language, and the interplay between form and meaning have left a lasting impact on literary criticism both within and beyond India. As we reflect on the historical development of Indian poetics, it becomes clear that this tradition offers invaluable insights into the universal qualities of literature and its capacity to shape human understanding across cultures and epochs.

CHAPTER THREE

EMOTIONAL LANDSCAPES

Emotions are the essence of human experience, and art has always been a powerful medium to express, evoke, and understand them. In both Indian and African cultures, narratives serve as vessels for exploring and conveying a wide range of emotions, making them an integral part of aesthetic expression. This chapter builds on the foundational concepts of aesthetic thought and focuses on the emotional dimensions of Indian and African narratives. By applying the Indian concept of *Rasa* to African literature, we will explore how emotions such as love, heroism, fear, compassion, and wonder are evoked in the works of African writers like Chinua Achebe, Chimamanda Ngozi Adichie, Buchi Emecheta, Mariama Bâ, and Ama Ata Aidoo. We will also examine how African concepts of emotion intersect with Indian aesthetic theory, offering new perspectives on the emotional landscapes within these cultural expressions.

Understanding Rasa: The Essence of Emotion

As discussed in the previous chapter, *Rasa* is a central concept in Indian aesthetics that refers to the emotional essence or flavor evoked by a work of art. According to Bharata Muni's *Natya Shastra*, *Rasa* arises from the interplay of determinants (*Vibhavas*), consequents (*Anubhavas*), and transitory emotional states (*Vyabhichari bhavas*), culminating in a transformative experience for the audience.

These emotions are universal in their appeal and relevance, making *Rasa* theory a valuable framework for analyzing literature across different cultures. By applying this theory to African narratives, we can gain deeper insights into the emotional landscapes they depict and understand how these emotions resonate with both local and universal experiences.

Emotional Landscapes in African Narratives

African literature, deeply rooted in oral traditions, often emphasizes emotional engagement, communal values, and moral lessons. The emotional landscapes portrayed in African narratives are rich and varied, reflecting the complexities of African societies and the human experience. The works of Chinua Achebe, Chimamanda Ngozi Adichie, Buchi Emecheta, Mariama Bâ, and Ama Ata Aidoo provide powerful examples of how emotions are woven into storytelling, making these narratives both compelling and thought-provoking.

1. Sringara (Love/Beauty) in African Narratives

Sringara, or the emotion of love and beauty, is a prominent theme in many African narratives. This Rasa is often explored through romantic relationships, familial bonds, and the connection to one's homeland and culture.

The exploration of Śṛṅgāra rasa (the aesthetic experience of love and beauty) within African narratives can offer a rich perspective, bridging Indian poetics with African literature. In classical Indian aesthetics, Śṛṅgāra represents both erotic love (Sambhoga Śṛṅgāra, love in union) and love in separation (Vipralambha Śṛṅgāra), often intertwined with beauty, nature, and emotional intensity. This concept can be effectively mapped onto African narratives that foreground love, beauty, and relationships, often within sociocultural and historical frameworks.

In Buchi Emecheta's *Second-Class Citizen*, the theme of love is intricately woven with identity, belonging, and struggle. The protagonist Adah's complex relationship with her husband Francis lacks the romantic Śṛṅgāra of fulfillment but resonates more with Vipralambha Śṛṅgāra (love in separation) due to emotional distance and power struggles. "Marriage was like a dream out of which one woke up drowning in a sea of loneliness."
(Buchi Emecheta, *Second-Class Citizen*). In this narrative, love is not romanticized but layered with complexities of race, gender, and colonial influence, where beauty is often tarnished by hardship. Yet, there is a subtle portrayal of feminine strength and the longing for beauty amidst struggle. Adah's beauty and desire for self-fulfillment represent a deeper search for identity and autonomy within a patriarchal and colonial framework.

In Chinua Achebe's *Things Fall Apart*, the beauty of Igbo traditions and the love for one's culture and community are central to the narrative. Okonkwo's attachment to his customs and his desire to maintain his cultural heritage reflects the emotion of *Sringara* on a societal level. The depiction of traditional rituals, festivals, and daily life in

Umuofia highlights the aesthetic beauty of Igbo culture. Achebe writes: "He has put a knife on the things that held us together and we have fallen apart" (Achebe, *Things Fall Apart*, p. 124). This line encapsulates the deep sense of loss and love for a way of life that is threatened by colonial forces. The beauty of the Igbo culture, intertwined with the love for its preservation, reflects *Sringara* in the context of cultural identity. Chinua Achebe's *Things Fall Apart*showcases love in its communal, familial, and spousal forms. While romantic love is not a central theme, some moments reflect cultural beauty and attraction. Okonkwo's wives, especially Ekwefi, portray a form of **Sambhoga Śṛṅgāra**, where love and beauty are expressed through admiration and shared experiences, but also through tensions, hardships, and loss. "Ekwefi had suffered a great deal in her life. She had borne ten children, and nine of them had died in infancy...It was her despair of ever having a living child that had led her to name her daughter Ezinma, 'the good one'" (Chinua Achebe, *Things Fall Apart*). Here, the beauty of the mother-daughter bond transcends romantic love, offering a glimpse of maternal love, a different facet of Śṛṅgāra.

In Ngũgĩ wa Thiong'o's *The River Between*, the central character Waiyaki's love for Nyambura is a classic portrayal of **Vipralambha Śṛṅgāra**, as their love is thwarted by sociopolitical divisions and cultural tensions. Their romance stands against a backdrop of colonialism and religious conflict, where the beauty of their love contrasts with the harsh reality of tribal divisions. "Nyambura was beautiful. Her beauty was not obvious at first glance; it was not the beauty of a girl who had been pampered and spoilt by the knowledge of her own attractiveness. Her beauty

was deeper, like the stillness of a windless night."
(Ngũgĩ wa Thiong'o, *The River Between*). Waiyaki and Nyambura's relationship reflects both the inner beauty of resistance and the longing for unity in a fragmented world.

African folktales, rich in cultural symbolism, often depict **Śṛṅgāra rasa** through the personification of nature and the beauty of relationships. In tales of kings, queens, and gods, the elements of love and beauty are often symbolic of harmony and disorder in the community. Love is often presented as a force that binds or fractures societies, and beauty is celebrated as a reflection of moral or spiritual purity. For example, in the Yoruba tale of Sango and Oya, the tempestuous relationship between the god of thunder and his wife Oya represents both love in union and in conflict, embodying Sambhoga and Vipralambha Śṛṅgāra through passion and betrayal. Their relationship reflects natural forces and the beauty and danger of love.

In Chimamanda Ngozi Adichie's *Americanah*, the love story between Ifemelu and Obinze showcases Sambhoga Śṛṅgāra, particularly in their initial romantic relationship and reunion. However, Adichie adds layers of social and political commentary, intertwining the theme of love with diaspora, race, and identity. "She rested her head against his chest. She had, finally, spun herself fully into his life, as if she had never been away" (Chimamanda Ngozi Adichie, *Americanah*). Their love story transcends continents and years, but is rooted in the beauty of cultural reconnection and personal discovery.

Chimamanda Ngozi Adichie's *Half of a Yellow Sun* explores *Sringara* through personal relationships, particularly the love story between Olanna and Odenigbo. Their love, tested by the harsh realities of the Nigerian Civil

War, is depicted with tenderness and complexity. Adichie portrays how love persists even in the face of turmoil and suffering, capturing the essence of *Sringara* in a modern African context: "She rested her head on his chest, feeling for the first time in a long time that things would be all right because he was there" (Adichie, *Half of a Yellow Sun*, p. 231). The novel portrays the beauty of personal love set against the backdrop of war, highlighting the enduring power of human connection and emotional resilience.

While African narratives might not always foreground romantic love in the same way classical Indian texts do, the essence of **Śṛṅgāra rasa**—love, beauty, longing, and emotional depth—exists through complex and multifaceted expressions of relationships. These narratives emphasize love amidst struggle, survival, and sociopolitical dynamics, often shifting between the union and separation inherent in Sambhoga and Vipralambha Śṛṅgāra.

2. Karuna (Compassion/Sorrow) in African Narratives

Karuna is the Rasa associated with compassion and sorrow, often evoked through themes of loss, suffering, and empathy. African literature frequently addresses social injustices, personal hardships, and collective tragedies, making *Karuna* a prevalent emotion. **Karuṇa rasa** plays a significant role in many African narratives, where stories of struggle, survival, and resistance are often intertwined with personal and communal grief. The emotional depth of compassion, empathy, and shared suffering reflects broader societal themes like colonialism, displacement, and social injustice.

In *Things Fall Apart*, **Karuṇa rasa** manifests in the downfall of **Okonkwo**, the protagonist, and the disintegration of his traditional Igbo society under the pressures of British colonialism and Christian missionary activities. Achebe creates a narrative steeped in sorrow and tragedy, as Okonkwo's suffering mirrors the collective anguish of his people. The deep sorrow in the novel arises from Okonkwo's inability to adapt to changing times. His rigid adherence to traditional masculinity and his fear of weakness lead to personal isolation, fractured relationships, and ultimately his downfall. "He has put a knife on the things that held us together and we have fallen apart" (Chinua Achebe, *Things Fall Apart*). Achebe taps into **Karuṇa rasa** through Okonkwo's final moments of despair when he realizes that his traditional values are no longer relevant, and his people are succumbing to colonial forces. Okonkwo's suicide is the ultimate act of sorrow, symbolizing both personal and communal loss, a failure of the old ways, and a deep compassion for the cultural erosion taking place.

Bessie Head's *A Question of Power* (1973) is a deeply personal novel that delves into the themes of mental illness, exile, and racial identity. The protagonist, Elizabeth, grapples with her inner demons while living in exile in Botswana, and through her, Head explores the overwhelming weight of sorrow and alienation. Karuna rasa is expressed in Elizabeth's suffering, as she battles with hallucinations and psychological breakdowns, which reflect her trauma of racial and cultural displacement. Her experiences of being a "half-caste" in apartheid South Africa contribute to her sense of sorrow, as she struggles with a fractured identity and a world that offers little compassion for her plight. "The weight of sorrow pressed upon her like a stone, making it difficult to breathe, and yet, in this pain, she saw a mirror of her fractured world."

Elizabeth's journey is not just one of personal sorrow but also empathy for the suffering of others. Bessie Head invites readers to feel compassion for a woman struggling against the crushing forces of colonialism, apartheid, and personal isolation, embodying Karuṇa rasa on multiple levels.

In Ben Okri's *The Famished Road* (1991), the novel centers on Azaro, a spirit child who exists between the worlds of the living and the dead. As he navigates the complexities of life in a post-colonial African village, the novel explores themes of suffering, poverty, and political corruption. Karuṇa rasa is deeply embedded in the depiction of Azaro's compassion for the people around him, who are trapped in cycles of despair and hunger. Okri's magical realism enhances the feeling of sorrow as Azaro witnesses the struggles of his family and his community. His mother and father work tirelessly to keep the family afloat, yet they face overwhelming challenges, from economic hardship to political violence. Azaro's father, in particular, becomes a tragic figure, representing the suffering of ordinary people under oppressive systems. "We are all hungry. We are all famished. The road is long, and the suffering endless, but we must keep walking." The Karuṇa rasa is intensified by the juxtaposition of the magical and the real, as Azaro's spirit-child nature allows him to see the deeper sorrows of the world. His empathy for the living and the dead reflects a broader compassion for the human condition, where survival is both a personal and communal struggle.

In *July's People* (1981), Nadine Gordimer presents a post-apartheid dystopian world where white South Africans are displaced from their positions of power and privilege. The novel follows the Smales family, who seek refuge with their Black servant, July, after a violent uprising. The sorrow in the novel comes from the inversion of social hierarchies and the collapse of societal norms.

The compassion that the reader is invited to feel is not only for the displaced white family but also for July, who must navigate his shifting roles between servant and protector. The novel explores the complexity of human relationships in a time of social upheaval, where old identities are destroyed, and new forms of suffering emerge. "There was sorrow in everything—the broken homes, the fractured loyalties, and the unspoken fears of a future that no one could yet comprehend." The Karuṇa rasa in *July's People* is tied to the deep emotional and psychological toll of living in a society on the verge of collapse. The novel invites readers to feel compassion for characters from different social backgrounds who are all grappling with the loss of their old lives and the uncertainty of what comes next.

In Buchi Emecheta's *Second Class Citizen*, the protagonist Adah's experiences of gender discrimination, racial prejudice, and personal struggles evoke deep compassion and empathy. Adah's journey as a Nigerian immigrant in Britain, facing numerous obstacles and striving for dignity and self-respect, elicits *Karuna* from the reader: "She felt as if she was standing on a precipice, the world around her dark and uncertain, but she would not give up; she would find a way, no matter what" (Emecheta, *Second Class Citizen*, p. 112). The narrative captures the sorrow and resilience of those marginalized by society, highlighting the universal need for compassion and understanding.

Mariama Bâ's *So Long a Letter* delves into *Karuna* through the emotional turmoil experienced by Ramatoulaye after the death of her husband and the betrayal of polygamy. The novel's epistolary form, a letter from Ramatoulaye to her friend Aissatou, reveals her inner sorrow and strength, evoking empathy for her situation: "I can no longer count the days when I have felt so alone, even when surrounded by people" (Bâ, *So Long a Letter*, p. 53). Through Ramatoulaye's sorrow, Bâ critiques societal norms and advocates for women's rights, making *Karuna* a vehicle for both emotional expression and social commentary.

In these works, **Karuṇa rasa** manifests in various forms, from the personal tragedies of characters like Okonkwo and Elizabeth to the communal sorrows of post-colonial societies grappling with identity, power, and survival. African narratives often deal with themes of displacement, cultural loss, and societal transformation, making **Karuṇa** a resonant emotional experience in many of these texts. The characters' struggles evoke deep empathy, whether it's Okonkwo's fall, Elizabeth's mental turmoil, or Azaro's compassionate witnessing of suffering in *The Famished Road*. These narratives show that compassion and sorrow are not isolated emotions but are tied to larger social, political, and historical forces shaping African societies.

3. Veera (Heroism) in African Narratives

Veera, or heroism, is a Rasa that celebrates bravery, courage, and strength in the face of adversity. African literature often portrays characters who embody these qualities, challenging oppression and striving for justice. African literature often highlights the struggles against colonialism, oppression, and societal challenges, making heroism a central theme in many works.

In Chinua Achebe's *Things Fall Apart*, Okonkwo's character is initially portrayed as the embodiment of *Veera*, admired for his strength, warrior skills, and leadership. His actions are driven by a desire to uphold his family's honor and the traditions of his community. However, Achebe complicates this heroic image by showing how Okonkwo's rigid adherence to traditional masculinity ultimately leads to his downfall: "His life had been ruled by a great passion—to become one of the lords of the clan. That had been his life-spring. And he had all but achieved it" (Achebe, *Things Fall Apart*, p. 131). Okonkwo's tragic fate reflects the tension between individual heroism and societal change, challenging traditional notions of heroism. In *Arrow of God*(1964), Ezeulu, the chief priest of Ulu, exemplifies **Vīra rasa** in his struggle to maintain the integrity of his traditional role and culture in the face of British colonialism and the imposition of Christianity. Ezeulu's heroic journey is marked by his refusal to surrender to colonial authority, even as it causes internal conflict and alienates him from his community. Achebe portrays Ezeulu as a complex hero, one whose actions are driven by both personal pride and a deep sense of responsibility to his people and their traditions. His steadfastness in protecting his spiritual duties reflects his heroism, but it also leads to tragic consequences. His resistance to colonial forces, particularly in his refusal to compromise his role as the intermediary between the gods and the people, is an expression of **Vīra rasa** in its more tragic form. "I am the arrow of my god, and my god has sent me to speak for him. Shall I betray him?" Ezeulu's heroism lies in his unwavering belief in his divine mission, even when it puts him at odds with both colonial officials and his own people. His struggle is emblematic of the broader resistance against colonial domination, a central theme in many African narratives.

In *A Grain of Wheat*(1967), Ngũgĩ Wa Thiong'O presents the Mau Mau Uprising in Kenya and the struggle for independence from British colonial rule. The novel examines heroism from multiple angles, focusing on characters who grapple with personal sacrifice, betrayal, and the collective fight for freedom. Mugo, the novel's central character, is initially seen as a hero, revered for his supposed act of courage in resisting the British. However, as the narrative unfolds, his inner conflicts reveal a more complex portrayal of heroism. While Mugo is ultimately revealed to be a flawed hero, **Kihika**, a Mau Mau rebel leader, represents the true spirit of **Vīra rasa**. Kihika's willingness to sacrifice his life for Kenya's freedom embodies the heroic ideal. His bravery, determination, and leadership in the face of overwhelming odds inspire others to join the struggle for independence. "He spoke of freedom, of the duty to fight. And they followed him because they saw in him the face of their own courage". Kihika's heroism is not only in his actions but also in his vision for a free Kenya. He becomes a symbol of resistance, embodying the spirit of the Mau Mau fighters who refused to accept subjugation.

Ama Ata Aidoo's *Changes: A Love Story* also portrays *Veera* through its protagonist Esi, who exhibits courage by defying societal expectations of marriage and gender roles. Esi's decision to divorce her husband and pursue her own independence is a radical act of heroism in a patriarchal society: "I will not be one of those women who put up with anything just to be married" (Aidoo, *Changes: A Love*

Story, p. 47). Esi's bravery challenges cultural norms and advocates for women's autonomy, highlighting the evolving nature of heroism in contemporary African society.

In *God's Bits of Wood* (1960), Sembene Ousmane presents a powerful narrative of heroism during the 1947–1948 railway strike in French West Africa. The novel chronicles the collective struggle of railway workers and their families against the French colonial authorities. The story's heroes are not just individuals but the entire community, including women and children, who rise up in the face of exploitation and oppression. Penda, a fearless woman leader, exemplifies Vīra rasa through her role in organizing the women's march. Despite being seen as unconventional and bold in a patriarchal society, Penda's courage and leadership are crucial to the success of the strike. She embodies the heroic spirit of resistance and defiance, even at great personal risk. "She led with her head held high, defiant against the injustice that had been dealt to them all." Penda's heroism, along with the collective strength of the strikers, highlights the theme of **Vīra rasa** as a communal experience. The novel shows that heroism is not limited to warriors or leaders, but can also be found in ordinary people fighting for their rights and dignity.

In *Maru* (1971), Margaret Cadmore, a Masarwa (Bushman) girl, represents a quiet form of heroism as she overcomes prejudice and marginalization in her society. The novel explores themes of racism, identity, and power, and while Margaret is not a traditional warrior, her quiet resilience in the face of systemic oppression embodies **Vīra rasa** in its more subtle form. Margaret's heroism is her refusal to be defined by her social status as a Masarwa, an underprivileged and oppressed group. Through her education and self-determination, she rises above the limitations placed on her by society. Her strength and resolve inspire others around her, including **Maru**, the chief, who sees her worth beyond her social status. "She had learned to carry her dignity like a cloak, unbroken by the prejudices of the world around her." Margaret's journey is one of personal heroism, challenging societal norms and asserting her identity with quiet but powerful determination.

Vīra rasa in African narratives manifests through characters who display bravery, resilience, and leadership, whether in direct combat against colonial forces or in more subtle acts of defiance against oppression and injustice. From **Kihika's** revolutionary zeal in *A Grain of Wheat*, to **Penda's** fearless leadership in *God's Bits of Wood*, to **Ezeulu's** spiritual heroism in *Arrow of God*, these characters reflect the heroic spirit that permeates much of African literature.

Heroism in these narratives is not limited to physical combat; it also includes intellectual, emotional, and moral courage. These works showcase how African authors have used **Vīra rasa** to highlight the various forms of resistance and resilience that define the continent's history and its people's quest for justice and dignity.

4. Bhayanaka (Fear) and Raudra (Anger) in African Narratives

Bhayanaka, or fear, and *Raudra*, or anger, are emotions that often surface in African narratives addressing themes of violence, oppression, and resistance. These emotions are central to portraying the psychological and social impact of colonialism, war, and inequality. In African narratives, where the horrors of colonialism, societal breakdown, and personal suffering often evoke fear and anger in characters and readers alike. These emotions are deeply intertwined with the historical and political contexts of oppression, violence, and resistance.

In *The Devil on the Cross* (1980), Ngũgĩ wa Thiong'o powerfully blends Bhayānaka and Raudra rasa to depict the horrors of post-colonial Kenya under the neocolonial bourgeoisie. The novel revolves around Wariinga, a young woman who experiences both fear and anger as she confronts the corruption and exploitation around her. Wariinga's fear stems from her powerlessness in a patriarchal, capitalistic society that abuses women and the working class.

Ngũgĩ captures Bhayānaka in Wariinga's early life, where she lives in constant fear of exploitation by wealthy, corrupt men. She becomes a symbol of the fear that ordinary Kenyans feel under the oppressive rule of neocolonial elites. "She felt her heart tighten, gripped by the cold hand of fear. The city was full of predators, waiting to feast on the weak." As the novel progresses, Wariinga's fear transforms into **Raudra rasa** (anger), when she recognizes the full extent of the exploitation and violence in her society. Her anger culminates in her taking a stand against the forces that oppress her, embodying a fierce resistance against the system. "The fire of rage burned in her chest, hot and unstoppable, a flame that would devour those who had built their power on the suffering of others." In Wariinga's journey from fear to anger, Ngũgĩ wa Thiong'o illustrates how fear can evolve into righteous anger, empowering individuals to fight back against unjust systems.

Anthills of the Savannah (1987) by Chinua Achebe explores the corrupt dictatorship in the fictional African country of Kangan. The novel portrays a society living under the constant threat of violence and repression, where fear (Bhayānaka) is ever-present. The story follows three central characters—Chris, Ikem, and Beatrice—who are involved in the political system, navigating the perils of a dictatorial regime. **Bhayānaka rasa** is palpable in the depiction of the general populace's fear of the military dictatorship. Achebe shows how the government's use of intimidation, censorship, and violence creates an atmosphere of pervasive fear. Characters are terrified of the unpredictable and brutal nature of the state's power. "The air was thick with the fear of what the soldiers might do next. Fear was the lifeblood of the regime, and it flowed through every corner of the land." As the narrative progresses, Raudra rasa emerges in the form of anger and rebellion. Ikem, a journalist, becomes the mouthpiece of the people's anger as he critiques the regime and speaks out against injustice. His defiance, though met with tragic consequences, sparks the flames of Raudra, highlighting the explosive potential of anger in the face of fear. "We must resist with all the anger that is in us, for anger is the fire that can consume tyranny." Achebe's portrayal of fear and anger in *Anthills of the Savannah* reflects the psychological and political tension in post-colonial African states, where fear of oppressive regimes often leads to bursts of revolutionary anger.

In Ayi Kwei Armah's *The Beautyful Ones Are Not Yet Born* (1968), Bhayānaka rasa is experienced through the protagonist's disillusionment with Ghana's corrupt post-independence government. The novel tells the story of a nameless man who struggles to maintain his integrity in a society rife with corruption and moral decay. Fear permeates the protagonist's life as he navigates a world where resisting corruption means risking social and financial ruin. **Bhayānaka** is evident in the atmosphere of dread that envelops the protagonist. He fears being ostracized by his peers and his family for refusing to participate in the corrupt practices that have become the norm. His fear reflects the broader societal fear of moral collapse and the consequences of integrity in a system that rewards dishonesty. "The stench of decay filled the air, and with it came the fear—the fear that nothing would ever change, that rot was all there was." As the protagonist becomes increasingly frustrated with the systemic corruption around him, his fear gives way to **Raudra rasa**—a deep, simmering anger directed at the political elite and the society that enables such corruption. His anger is quiet but profound, reflecting the suppressed rage of those who refuse to compromise their morals in the face of overwhelming pressure. "A fierce anger bubbled up within him, not the anger that shouts but the kind that festers in silence, burning a hole through everything it touches." In *The Beautyful Ones Are Not Yet Born*, Armah explores how fear can give rise to anger, and how that anger can either be suppressed or serve as a quiet form of resistance against corruption and moral decay.

Amos Tutuola's *The Palm-Wine Drinkard* (1952) is a surreal, mythological journey that blends the fantastical with the terrifying. The novel follows the adventures of the Drinkard, who embarks on a quest to bring back his dead palm wine tapster. Along the way, he encounters a series of strange, fearsome creatures and situations that evoke

Bhayānaka rasa. The novel's exploration of the supernatural world is filled with moments of fear and dread, as the Drinkard faces monstrous beings, dark spirits, and otherworldly trials. Bhayānaka is expressed through the eerie and threatening atmosphere of the Drinkard's journey, as he navigates the unknown and the uncontrollable forces of the spirit world. "I stood still, rooted by the terror that gripped my heart as the monstrous figure loomed before me, a grotesque vision of all my fears made flesh. Through its folkloric narrative, *The Palm-Wine Drinkard* creates a world of supernatural fear, where **Bhayānaka rasa** dominates the protagonist's encounters with the unknown.

In Chimamanda Ngozi Adichie's *Half of a Yellow Sun*, the Nigerian Civil War and its devastating effects evoke *Bhayanaka* and *Raudra*. The fear experienced by the characters in the face of bombings, starvation, and loss is palpable, reflecting the broader fear felt by the entire community. Ugwu's experiences as a young boy conscripted into the army and his exposure to the horrors of war vividly capture *Bhayanaka*: "The fear settled in his stomach like a heavy stone, and he knew that nothing would ever be the same again" (Adichie, *Half of a Yellow Sun*, p. 312). Similarly, *Raudra* is expressed through the characters' anger towards the injustice and violence they face. Adichie portrays how anger becomes a catalyst for resistance and activism, urging readers to recognize the moral imperative of opposing oppression.

Buchi Emecheta's *The Joys of Motherhood* also depicts *Bhayanaka* and *Raudra* through the experiences of Nnu Ego, whose life is marked by constant struggle and hardship. Her anger at societal expectations and her fear for her children's future reflect broader concerns about the roles of women and the pressures of traditional expectations: "Her anger was like a wave, rising and crashing, sweeping away the foundations of her life" (Emecheta, *The Joys of Motherhood*, p. 180). These emotions provide insight into the psychological impact of social and cultural constraints, highlighting the need for empathy and understanding.

Bhayānaka rasa and Raudra rasa often go hand in hand in African narratives, as fear of oppressive systems, violence, or moral decay frequently leads to righteous anger and rebellion. In novels like *The Devil on the Cross* and *Anthills of the Savannah*, characters first experience fear under tyrannical regimes before their anger drives them toward resistance and rebellion. **Ayi Kwei** Armah's protagonist in *The Beautyful Ones Are Not Yet Born* experiences a quieter but equally powerful blend of fear and anger, as he resists the temptations of a corrupt society.

In more fantastical works like Amos Tutuola's *The Palm-Wine Drinkard*, Bhayānaka rasa is presented through the fear of the unknown, as characters navigate eerie, supernatural landscapes.

Emotional landscapes in African Igbo tradition

The emotional landscape of the Igbo people, one of Nigeria's largest ethnic groups, is characterized by a rich tapestry of cultural beliefs, values, and practices that shape individual and communal identities. This emotional framework is rooted in traditional customs, spiritual beliefs, and social structures that reflect the interplay between personal emotions and collective experiences. Understanding this landscape involves exploring various dimensions, including family dynamics, spirituality, communal ties, and the significance of rituals, language, and folklore.

At the heart of Igbo emotional expression is the concept of *Umunna*, which signifies a broader sense of kinship and community. This principle asserts that an individual's identity is intricately linked to their family and community. Consequently, emotions such as joy, grief, and pride are communal experiences rather than merely personal feelings. For instance, during traditional ceremonies like weddings or naming ceremonies, the joy of the family extends to the entire village. The community's involvement in these celebrations not only amplifies the emotional impact but also reinforces social bonds and shared cultural heritage. Similarly, during times of mourning, the entire community participates in rituals to honor the deceased, demonstrating solidarity and shared grief. This collective emotional experience emphasizes the Igbo belief that individual well-being is deeply intertwined with communal harmony.

The significance of spirituality in shaping the Igbo emotional landscape cannot be overstated. The Igbo worldview is deeply rooted in the belief in a spiritual dimension that influences everyday life. The concept of *chi*, representing the personal god or spiritual essence of an individual, plays a critical role in determining one's fate and emotional state. The relationship with one's *chi* influences feelings of happiness, fulfillment, or misfortune. Emotions are thus not seen in isolation; rather, they are understood in the context of one's spiritual life. The Igbo people often engage in rituals and prayers to connect with their *chi* and seek guidance or intervention during challenging times. These spiritual practices underscore the belief that emotions can transcend the individual, linking personal experiences to the broader spiritual universe.

Traditional rituals and ceremonies are vital expressions of the emotional landscape in Igbo culture. Festivals like the New Yam Festival (*Iri Ji*) are pivotal in reinforcing communal bonds and shared emotions. This festival, which celebrates the harvest and expresses gratitude to the earth goddess and ancestors, is marked by communal feasting, dancing, and performances. The act of sharing food symbolizes abundance and unity, creating a sense of belonging among community members. Similarly, the *Ekpe* and *Masquerade* festivals, which involve traditional dances and rituals, evoke feelings of pride, cultural identity, and communal solidarity. Such festivals not only serve as a means of expressing joy but also reinforce social structures and cultural norms.

Igbo proverbs, folklore, and storytelling are essential vehicles for conveying emotional wisdom and moral lessons within the community. Proverbs often encapsulate complex emotions and social truths in concise phrases, guiding interpersonal relationships and ethical conduct. For example, the saying, "He who does not cultivate his farm will die of hunger," underscores the values of hard work and foresight, while also invoking feelings of responsibility and communal interdependence. Folktales often feature characters who navigate emotional challenges, offering insights into human behavior and societal values. These narratives provide a framework for understanding emotions like love, jealousy, and anger, illustrating how they can lead to both positive outcomes and personal conflicts.

The role of family in shaping emotional dynamics is paramount in Igbo society. The family unit is viewed as the cornerstone of social life, where relationships are built on mutual respect and responsibility. Parental love is expressed through nurturing, guidance, and discipline. For instance, a mother's affection for her children is often intertwined with expectations for them to contribute to the family's well-being and uphold cultural values. In return, children are expected to show respect and loyalty to their parents, reinforcing emotional bonds. This reciprocal relationship emphasizes the importance of emotional support within the family, highlighting the interconnectedness of individual emotions and family dynamics.

Additionally, the emotional landscape is influenced by gender roles and expectations within Igbo society. Traditionally, men are seen as providers and protectors, while women are often associated with nurturing and community-building. These roles shape emotional expressions and interactions, leading to different expectations for how men and women experience and communicate their feelings. While traditional gender roles may impose certain limitations on emotional expression, there is also a recognition of the fluidity of these roles in contemporary contexts. As gender dynamics evolve, so too does the expression of emotions, leading to a more nuanced understanding of emotional experiences in modern Igbo life.

Moreover, the impact of globalization and modernity on the emotional landscape of the Igbo people cannot be overlooked. As urbanization and migration increase, traditional practices and beliefs are sometimes challenged by external influences. Young people may grapple with the tension between preserving cultural identity and adapting to contemporary values. This tension can lead to a re-evaluation of emotional expressions and connections to community, family, and tradition. Despite these changes, many Igbo people continue to find ways to integrate traditional values with modern experiences, seeking to maintain emotional ties to their heritage while navigating new social landscapes.

Language also plays a crucial role in expressing emotions within Igbo culture. The richness of the Igbo language, with its tonal nuances and proverbs, allows for a wide range of emotional expression. The use of metaphor and imagery in Igbo poetry and songs captures the depth of human emotions and experiences. Music, in particular, serves as a powerful medium for expressing feelings, whether through traditional songs that recount historical events or contemporary music that addresses social issues. The emotional power of music in Igbo culture is undeniable, as it can evoke feelings of nostalgia, joy, and communal solidarity.

Furthermore, the interrelationship between emotions and nature is significant in Igbo tradition. The environment is not merely a backdrop for human activity; it is imbued with spiritual significance and emotional resonance. The natural world—trees, rivers, and mountains—is often personified and seen as a source of wisdom, guidance, and emotional support. Many Igbo proverbs highlight the importance of nature in shaping emotional experiences, such as the saying, "A child who is not embraced by the village will burn it down to feel its warmth," illustrating the deep connection between individual emotions and communal relationships with nature.

In essence, the emotional landscape in Igbo tradition is a rich and intricate tapestry that reflects the interplay of individual and communal experiences, spirituality, and cultural identity. Emotions are not isolated phenomena; they are embedded within a broader framework of beliefs, values, and practices that shape how individuals relate to themselves, their families, and their communities. This emotional richness underscores the resilience of the Igbo people and their capacity to navigate the complexities of life while remaining connected to their cultural heritage.

As the Igbo continue to evolve in a rapidly changing world, their emotional landscape remains a vital aspect of their identity, grounding them in their history while also allowing for adaptation and growth. The celebration of shared emotions, the integration of traditional and modern values, and the acknowledgment of the spiritual dimensions of life ensure that the essence of the Igbo emotional landscape endures, offering insights into the universal human experience of emotion and connection.

In conclusion, the emotional landscape of the Igbo people is a testament to the intricate connections between individuals, families, communities, and the spiritual world. It illustrates how emotions are not merely personal experiences but are deeply rooted in cultural practices, social norms, and shared beliefs. As the Igbo navigate their identities in an increasingly globalized world, their emotional landscape will continue to evolve, reflecting both the enduring power of tradition and the transformative potential of contemporary experiences.

The intersection of Indian and African Emotional Theories

The intersection of Indian emotional theories and African emotional narratives offers a rich comparative framework for understanding human experience and expression across cultures. Both traditions have developed intricate systems to explore emotions (known as *rasa* in Indian aesthetics and various emotional states in African narratives), but they emerge from different philosophical, historical, and cultural contexts.

In Indian aesthetics, emotions are central to the *rasa* theory, elaborated in texts such as Bharata Muni's *Nāṭyaśāstra* and expanded by later scholars like Ānandavardhana and Abhinavagupta. Meanwhile, African narratives, informed by oral traditions, mythology, colonial histories, and postcolonial realities, also express a wide range of emotions, often rooted in communal experiences, storytelling, and resistance against oppression.

The application of *Rasa* theory to African narratives reveals a rich interplay between Indian and African aesthetic thought. While *Rasa* provides a structured framework for understanding emotions, African literature offers a more fluid and contextual approach, deeply rooted in communal values, oral traditions, and historical experiences. This intersection allows for a nuanced analysis of how emotions are portrayed, understood, and experienced across different cultural contexts. Key aspects of *rasa* theory:

1. Bhāva (emotion or mood) is the foundational emotional state that triggers the *rasa* in the audience.
2. Vibhāva (determinants) are the causes or stimuli that lead to the emotion.
3. Anubhāva (consequent reactions) are the physical or psychological manifestations of the emotion.
4. Vyabhicāribhāva (transitory emotions) are fleeting emotions that enhance the main emotion.

The aim of art in this framework is to evoke these *rasas* in the audience, thereby leading to a heightened state of awareness, pleasure, or insight.

In African narratives, emotions are often portrayed not just as individual experiences but as collective ones, reflecting the interconnectedness of community life. The communal aspect of African emotional expression resonates with the concept of *Sahridaya* in Indian aesthetics, which refers to the shared aesthetic experience between the artist and the audience. This communal aspect deepens the emotional engagement, making the narratives more impactful and relatable. In African narratives, emotions are deeply intertwined with historical realities, cultural practices, and oral traditions. Unlike the formalized *rasa* theory in Indian aesthetics, emotions in African literature and oral storytelling often focus on:

1. Communal Experience: African emotional expression is often rooted in the collective experience of the community. The emotional responses in narratives are deeply linked to communal joys, sorrows, struggles, and triumphs.
2. Resistance and Survival: Emotions in African literature often emerge from resistance to colonialism, apartheid, slavery, and various forms of oppression. Fear, anger, and heroism are frequently explored in narratives of struggle.
3. Interpersonal and Familial Dynamics: Love, sorrow, and compassion in African literature are frequently conveyed through familial ties, community bonds, and relationships.

Although there isn't a singular system like *rasa* theory in African aesthetics, emotions in African narratives are conveyed through oral storytelling techniques, traditional music, dance, and rituals, all of which evoke strong emotional responses in participants.

The exploration of emotional landscapes in Indian and African narratives through the lens of *Rasa* theory offers valuable insights into the universal nature of human emotions and the cultural specificity of their expression. By examining how emotions like love, compassion, heroism, fear, and anger are depicted in the works of African writers, we gain a deeper understanding of the cultural and historical contexts that shape these narratives. This comparative analysis enriches our appreciation of both Indian and African aesthetic traditions, highlighting their capacity to evoke powerful emotional responses and foster a deeper understanding of the human condition.

When examining Indian and African emotional theories side by side, several areas of intersection and dialogue become evident: **Śṛṅgāra rasa** focuses on both romantic love and aesthetic beauty in Indian narratives. It often explores the emotions that arise from the union or separation of lovers, and the beauty of nature or art. In African narratives, love is frequently depicted through familial, communal, and romantic relationships, often contextualized by hardship, colonial disruption, or societal norms. For example, in Mariama Bâ's *So Long a Letter*, love between friends and within family circles is explored, as well as the tensions and beauty in love under the strain of polygamy. Both traditions explore the depths of human relationships, the tension between personal desire and societal expectations, and the role of love in personal and communal fulfillment. However, while *Śṛṅgāra* in Indian texts often deals with romantic love, African texts may emphasize communal or familial love, set against the backdrop of societal struggles.

Karuṇa rasa in Indian aesthetics focuses on compassion and sorrow, often in response to the suffering of others or tragic events. Sorrow is a central theme in African narratives, particularly in postcolonial literature, where the trauma of colonization, slavery, and apartheid has left indelible emotional scars. Buchi Emecheta's *The Joys of Motherhood* reflects on the sorrow of Nnu Ego, who grapples with the challenges of motherhood in a colonial society that undermines traditional values. Both Indian and African narratives deeply explore the universality of sorrow and loss, whether it is due to personal tragedy or societal collapse. *Karuṇa rasa* resonates with the empathetic portrayal of suffering in African literature, where characters often evoke compassion from the reader through their hardships and resilience.

Vīra rasa in Indian aesthetics emphasizes valor, courage, and heroism, often celebrated in epics like the *Mahābhārata* and *Rāmāyaṇa*. African narratives frequently celebrate heroic resistance to colonial rule, oppression, and systemic injustice. In Ngũgĩ wa Thiong'o's *A Grain of Wheat*, characters like Kihika embody heroism as they fight for Kenya's independence. Similarly, in Sembene Ousmane's *God's Bits of Wood*, the collective heroism of the Senegalese railway workers in their fight against French colonial rule exemplifies Vīra. The concept of heroism in both traditions is linked to acts of courage, often in the face of overwhelming odds. In Indian aesthetics, heroism is idealized in mythical or royal figures, while in African narratives, it is often rooted in ordinary people fighting for justice and freedom.

Bhayānaka rasa in Indian aesthetics captures the emotion of fear, often evoked through situations of danger, the supernatural, or moral peril. Fear in African narratives frequently arises from real-world dangers—such as violence, political instability, and the horrors of slavery and colonialism. Amos Tutuola's *The Palm-Wine Drinkard* blends the supernatural and real-world fears as the protagonist journeys through a world filled with eerie spirits and dangerous entities. Both traditions explore fear as a powerful and universal human emotion. In Indian texts, *Bhayānaka* often deals with existential or supernatural threats, while in African literature, fear is grounded in historical and political realities but may also involve elements of the supernatural.

Raudra rasa in Indian aesthetics represents wrath and righteous anger, often linked to the idea of justice and moral outrage. In African narratives, anger is frequently directed at colonial and postcolonial systems of oppression. In Chinua Achebe's *Things Fall Apart*, the protagonist Okonkwo's anger represents his resistance to the encroachment of British colonial rule and the breakdown of traditional Igbo society. Both traditions treat anger as a complex and often destructive force, but also as a response to injustice. Indian aesthetics channel anger through divine or heroic figures, while African literature often portrays anger as a response to historical wrongs, such as colonization and systemic racism.

The intersection of Indian and African emotional theories offers a fascinating study of human emotion as both a personal and collective experience. In Indian aesthetics, emotions are codified into a formal system through *rasa*, while African narratives often explore emotions through storytelling, oral tradition, and lived historical experiences.

Despite their different origins, both traditions emphasize the transformative power of emotions, whether it's the valor and courage of heroes, the sorrow of oppressed communities, or the righteous anger of those resisting injustice. Through their respective frameworks, Indian and African emotional theories reflect the diverse ways in which humanity confronts the beauty, joy, suffering, and injustice of life.

The exploration of **Emotional Landscapes** in both Indian and African narratives reveals a profound intersection of human emotions, illustrating how different cultural, historical, and aesthetic frameworks converge to portray universal emotional experiences. In this chapter, we have examined how the Indian concept of **rasa**—a sophisticated theory of emotional aesthetics—finds resonances in the emotional expressions embedded within African storytelling traditions. Despite the vast geographical, cultural, and historical differences, both traditions share a commitment to evoking deep emotional responses, be it through the depiction of love, sorrow, heroism, fear, or anger.

Indian aesthetic theory, particularly the *Navarasa*, provides a formalized system for understanding and categorizing emotions. These nine *rasas*—**Śṛṅgāra** (love), **Karuṇa** (sorrow), **Vīra** (heroism), **Bhayānaka** (fear), **Raudra** (anger), **Hāsya** (humor), **Bībhatsa** (disgust), **Adbhuta** (wonder), and **Śānta** (peace)—serve as a powerful framework for interpreting the emotional dimensions of narratives. Rooted in classical Sanskrit aesthetics, this system underscores the role of art and literature in cultivating and refining the emotional sensibilities of its audience. The interplay of **bhāva** (the emotional state), **vibhāva** (the cause or stimulus of emotion), and **anubhāva** (the reaction or response) is central to how emotions are produced and experienced.

On the other hand, African narratives—shaped by the legacies of colonialism, oral traditions, community-based storytelling, and resistance—approach emotions from a more contextual and experiential standpoint. In African literature, emotions such as love, sorrow, fear, anger, and heroism are often intertwined with the collective struggles and triumphs of communities. The emotional responses of characters and readers alike are deeply rooted in the socio-political landscapes of African societies, where historical traumas like slavery, colonization, and apartheid have left a lasting impact on emotional expression. The emotions explored in African literature are not only individual experiences but also collective expressions of resistance, survival, and hope.

The convergence of these two traditions allows us to understand emotions as a universal, yet contextually shaped, phenomenon. While Indian aesthetics provides a structured, almost scientific approach to the evocation of emotions, African narratives emphasize the lived, raw, and communal nature of emotional experiences. This contrast highlights the importance of cultural context in shaping emotional expression, yet it also points to the universality of certain emotional experiences. Both traditions celebrate the depth of human emotions, whether through the stylized representation of **Śṛṅgāra** and **Karuṇa** in Indian texts or through the visceral depictions of love, sorrow, and heroism in African literature.

Moreover, this comparative analysis sheds light on the emotional complexity within postcolonial African narratives, where the **Bhayānaka** of fear and **Raudra** of anger are intimately connected with the historical realities of oppression and liberation struggles. The **Vīra** of African heroes parallels the valor celebrated in Indian epics, but it is reframed in the context of political resistance and the fight for justice in a world shaped by colonialism.

In conclusion, the study of **Emotional Landscapes** across Indian and African narratives offers a unique lens through which we can explore the emotional dimensions of literature and human experience. It allows us to appreciate the diverse ways in which cultures express emotions while recognizing the shared emotional truths that transcend cultural boundaries. Whether through the highly aestheticized emotions of Indian *rasa* theory or the grounded, historically informed emotions of African storytelling, both traditions ultimately lead us to a deeper understanding of the human emotional experience. The intersection of these emotional landscapes enriches our perception of the role emotions play in shaping narratives, identities, and collective memories, providing a holistic view of the emotional undercurrents that define literature across time and place.

PERFORMANCE AND PARTICIPATION

In Indian and African cultures, performance serves as a dynamic means of artistic expression and cultural communication. Performance traditions, encompassing dance, music, theater, and ritual, are integral to communal life and are often seen as embodiments of cultural values, historical memory, and spiritual beliefs. This chapter explores the role of performance in Indian and African traditions, focusing on how these practices foster participation and engagement. By examining Indian classical dance and theater alongside African music and dance rituals, this chapter seeks to understand how performance as a cultural act enhances the aesthetic experience and deepens the emotional and spiritual connections to the presented narratives. Participation—whether as performers or audience members—plays a crucial role in creating a shared aesthetic experience, that entertains, educates, preserves cultural heritage, and fosters social cohesion.

Performance, in both Indian and African cultures, is far more than a form of entertainment; it is an essential means of expressing identity, spirituality, and community values. Across these vast and diverse regions, performance encompasses an array of art forms—including dance, music, theater, oral storytelling, and ritual practices—that not only reflect cultural heritage but also engage audiences in deeply participatory ways. The concept of participation-performance, where the audience is invited to actively engage with the performance, plays a central role in fostering emotional, spiritual, and social unity.

In India, performance is grounded in ancient aesthetic traditions like the *Nātyaṣāstra*, which established the theoretical framework for evoking specific emotions (rasa) in the audience. Dance forms like Bharatanatyam, Kathak, and Odissi, along with folk traditions such as Therukoothu and Garba, serve as vehicles for conveying moral and spiritual narratives. Similarly, religious festivals such as Durga Puja and Ramlila invite entire communities to participate, blending performance with ritual in ways that strengthen social bonds and collective identity.

African performance traditions, though different in their historical and cultural origins, share a similar emphasis on the integration of performance and participation. Oral storytelling, dance, and music in Africa are often communal experiences, with performances designed to invoke not only the physical presence of the audience but also their emotional and spiritual participation. Whether it is through the dynamic call-and-response techniques in storytelling or the rhythmic collective energy in African dance, these performances transcend mere entertainment, becoming tools for educating, uniting, and preserving the cultural values of the community.

At the heart of performance in both Indian and African traditions is the idea of emotional resonance—a shared journey where performers and participants co-create an experience that transcends the boundaries of performer and spectator. This concept is essential to understanding the participatory nature of these performances. In India, the evocation of specific rasas like Śṛṅgāra (love) and Karuṇa (compassion) invites the audience to become emotionally involved, while in Africa, the emphasis on collective storytelling and music fosters a sense of shared emotion and purpose.

While the aesthetic, spiritual, and cultural frameworks of Indian and African performance traditions differ in significant ways, they converge in their emphasis on community, participation, and emotional engagement. In both regions, performance is not a one-sided act of artistic display but an inclusive, participatory event where meaning is co-created between the performer and the audience. This chapter explores the intricacies of these traditions, focusing on how performance and participation-performance function within Indian and African cultural contexts, highlighting their social, spiritual, and emotional significance.

In delving into this comparative study, we will examine the following key aspects:

- The role of performance as a cultural and spiritual conduit in both Indian and African societies.

- The participatory elements of performance that blur the boundaries between performer and audience.
- The ways in which performance serves as a means of social cohesion and cultural transmission in both traditions.

By exploring these themes, this chapter seeks to provide a comprehensive understanding of how performance and participation intersect in Indian and African cultures, revealing the deep connections between art, spirituality, and community life across these diverse regions.

Performance in Indian Culture

India's rich performance traditions have evolved over thousands of years, deeply influenced by religious, philosophical, and cultural beliefs. From classical dance forms like Bharatanatyam and Kathak to the theatrical traditions of Sanskrit drama, Indian performance arts are deeply intertwined with concepts of *Rasa* (emotional flavor), *Bhava* (expression), and *Natya* (drama). Performance in Indian culture is not merely an act of entertainment but a sacred ritual that seeks to connect the human with the divine, the physical with the metaphysical.

Performance in Indian culture is a multifaceted expression of art, spirituality, and social life, deeply embedded in the country's ancient traditions and philosophies. From classical dance forms and music to folk theater and religious rituals, Indian performance traditions are rich in symbolism, rooted in religious texts, and governed by codified aesthetic principles. Central to Indian performance is the concept of **participation**, where the audience is not merely a spectator but an active participant in the emotional and spiritual journey created by the performance.

The Theoretical Foundation: Nāṭyaśāstra and Rasa Theory

At the core of Indian performance traditions is the *Nātyaṣāstra*, an ancient Sanskrit text attributed to Bharata Muni, written around 200 BCE to 200 CE. It serves as the foundational treatise on drama, dance, and music, outlining the aesthetic and technical aspects of performance. According to the *Nātyaṣāstra*, performance is a means of conveying emotions (bhāva) to evoke specific emotional responses, called rasas, in the audience.

The **rasa theory** is central to Indian performance. The nine rasas—**Śṛṅgāra** (love), **Vīra** (heroism), **Karuṇa** (compassion), **Raudra** (anger), **Bhayānaka** (fear), **Bībhatsa** (disgust), **Adbhuta** (wonder), **Hāsya** (laughter), and **Śānta** (peace)—represent a spectrum of human emotions. The performer aims to create a vivid experience for the audience, allowing them to experience these emotions deeply. This interaction between the performer's expression (bhāva) and the audience's emotional response (rasa) forms the crux of Indian performance.

1. Indian Classical Dance

Indian classical dance forms such as Bharatanatyam, Kathak, Odissi, and Kathakali are highly stylized and codified, with roots in ancient scriptures like the *Natya Shastra*. These dance forms emphasize the use of *Abhinaya* (expressive acting) to convey emotional states and narrative elements. Bharatanatyam, for example, employs facial expressions, hand gestures (*mudras*), and body movements to tell stories from Hindu mythology, often portraying themes of love, devotion, and heroism.

The concept of *Rasa* is central to Indian classical dance, with the dancer striving to evoke specific emotions in the audience. As Bharata Muni states in the *Natya Shastra*: "Rasa is created from a combination of the determinants (vibhava), the consequents (anubhava), and the transitory states (vyabhichari bhava)" (Bharata Muni, *Natya Shastra*, p. 54). Through the dancer's skillful portrayal, the audience experiences *Rasa*, becoming emotionally engaged and aesthetically fulfilled. This engagement is not passive; the audience is considered an active participant, whose response completes the aesthetic experience.

Indian classical dance is an intricate blend of **aesthetics**, **spirituality**, and **storytelling**. The tradition draws from the ancient treatise **Nāṭyaśāstra**, which codifies the forms and functions of dance, drama, and music. At the heart of this tradition are the **four types of Abhinaya** (expressions) used by dancers to communicate emotions and tell stories:

1. **Āṅgikābhinaya**: Physical gestures.
2. **Vācikābhinaya**: Verbal expression, including the music and lyrics.
3. **Āhāryābhinaya**: Costumes, makeup, and accessories.
4. **Sāttvikābhinaya**: The internal, emotional expression that comes from within, showing the dancer's psychological state.

These elements create an integrated experience that communicates emotions (bhāvas) and evokes specific rasas (emotional states) in the audience.

1.1. Bharatanātyam: Grace and Geometric Precision

Bharatanātyam is one of India's most ancient and revered classical dance forms, originating from Tamil Nadu. It was initially performed in temples as a form of spiritual offering. Bharatanātyam is characterized by its precise footwork, expressive gestures, and intricate facial expressions.

Bharatanātyam

The physical movements of Bharatanātyam are highly structured. The dancer's body, particularly the **Mudras** (hand gestures), plays a critical role in storytelling. The posture of **Araimandi** (half-seated position) is a foundational stance that combines strength and grace. Dancers also perform rhythmic footwork called **Tattadavu**. The vocal component comes from the **Carnatic music** accompaniment and the lyrics that narrate the stories. Although the dancers doesn't speak, they communicate through lip synchronization and rhythmic syllables (jatis) while expressing emotions through abhinaya. Bharatanātyam dancers wear vibrant silk saris that are stitched for easy movement, with temple jewelry, **ghungroos** (ankle bells), and elaborate makeup that highlights facial expressions, especially around the eyes. The portrayal of internal emotions, where the dancer must convey spiritual and emotional depth, such as love, devotion, or compassion. A dancer must embody a deity or hero to move the audience beyond the physical into the spiritual realm.

1.2. Kathak: Storytelling through Rhythm and Grace

Kathak, originating from North India, is a dance form known for its fast spins, rhythmic footwork, and storytelling gestures. It blends Hindu temple traditions and Persian court influences from the Mughal era.

Kathak

- **Āṅgikābhinaya**: Kathak's distinguishing feature is its rapid, rhythmic footwork known as **tatkaar**. Dancers use their hands, head, and eyes to convey complex narratives with minimal movement. The spins, or **chakkars**, are graceful and hypnotic, enhancing the drama of the storytelling.
- **Vācikābhinaya**: Kathak often includes rhythmic syllables recited by the dancer or spoken by the accompanying tabla or harmonium player. The music is predominantly **Hindustani classical** and the lyrics are typically devotional or romantic, drawn from poets like **Mirabai** or **Tulsidas**.

- **Āhāryābhinaya**: Costumes in Kathak are inspired by Mughal attire. Women wear flowing **Anarkali** dresses or lehengas, while men wear kurtas. The **ghungroos** (ankle bells) are central to the performance, accentuating the footwork.
- **Sāttvikābhinaya**: Kathak dancers must evoke deep emotions like longing, devotion, or mischief through their subtle facial expressions. The dancer connects emotionally with the audience, transcending physical gestures to embody the spirit of the characters they portray.

1.3 Mohiniyattam: The Dance of the Enchantress

Mohiniyattam, also from Kerala, is known for its graceful and sensuous movements. It draws from **Lasya**, the feminine aspect of dance, and is performed in honor of **Mohini**, the female avatar of Vishnu.

Mohiniyāttam

- **Āṅgikābhinaya**: Mohiniyattam is characterized by soft, flowing movements of the body and arms, with gentle swaying and delicate footwork. The dance has a slow tempo, emphasizing grace and femininity.
- **Vācikābhinaya**: The accompanying music is in **Carnatic style**, with lyrics often in **Manipravalam** (a mixture of Sanskrit and Malayalam). The lyrical content is devotional, focusing on themes of love and spirituality.
- **Āhāryābhinaya**: Mohiniyattam dancers wear a white and gold-bordered sari, with simple jewelry and minimal makeup to maintain the natural beauty of the performer. The simplicity of the costume contrasts with the richness of the performance.
- **Sāttvikābhinaya**: The dancer must evoke delicate emotions like love, devotion, and longing. The internalization of these feelings, and their expression

1.4. Odissi: The Dance of Grace and Devotion

Odissi is one of the classical dance forms of India, originating from the eastern state of Odisha. Known for its fluid movements, intricate footwork, and expressive gestures, Odissi is deeply rooted in the devotional practices of Hinduism, particularly in the worship of Lord Jagannath. The dance is characterized by its unique style of body postures and the use of **Mudras** (hand gestures) to convey emotions and narratives.

odissi

Āṅgikābhinaya in Odissi involves intricate body movements that combine grace and strength.

- **Postures**: Odissi features a distinctive stance called **Chowka** and **Bhangas**. Chowka is a square stance that emphasizes strength, often associated with male deities, while Bhangas, characterized by a more curvilinear posture, emphasizes femininity and is often associated with female deities.
- **Footwork**: The footwork in Odissi is rhythmic and involves **Hasta Mudras** (hand gestures) that are coordinated with the foot movements, allowing the dancer to create complex rhythmic patterns. The movements often follow the rhythmic cycles of the music, enhancing the overall aesthetic of the

performance.

- **Expressiveness**: The use of upper body movements combined with lower body positioning allows for nuanced storytelling. The torso plays an important role, with movements flowing gracefully while maintaining a strong connection to the ground.

Vācikābhinaya in Odissi involves the integration of lyrical content with the dance.

- **Accompaniment**: The dance is performed to the accompaniment of **Odissi music**, which includes vocal and instrumental components. Traditional **Chhanda** (poetic verses) and **Shloka** (sacred verses) are often sung, enhancing the spiritual aspect of the performance.
- **Narrative Themes**: The themes explored in Odissi are often drawn from Hindu mythology and devotional poetry, especially focusing on the life and exploits of Lord Krishna and the gopis (milkmaids). The dancer conveys these narratives through expressive gestures and facial expressions, using **Abhinaya** to bring the stories to life.

Āhāryābhinaya in Odissi is characterized by its beautiful costumes and makeup.

- **Costumes**: Odissi dancers typically wear a traditional costume made of silk, adorned with intricate patterns and vibrant colors. The attire includes a **sari** draped in a specific style, accentuating the dancer's movements. The **Odissi sari** is often paired with a **choli** (blouse) and a **sash** (uchchhishta) that holds the drape in place.

- **Jewelry**: The jewelry is elaborate, including necklaces, earrings, and **armlets**, all made of gold or imitation jewelry, enhancing the overall visual appeal of the performance.
- **Makeup**: The makeup is designed to highlight the dancer's facial features, particularly the eyes, which are emphasized to express emotions and connect with the audience. The use of kohl (black eyeliner) creates a dramatic effect, allowing for deep expressions.

Sāttvikābhinaya in Odissi focuses on the internal emotional expressions of the dancer.

- **Emotional Depth**: Dancers in Odissi must internalize and express a range of emotions. from joy and love to devotion and longing. This internalization is conveyed through subtle changes in facial expressions, particularly in the eyes and mouth, which form the essence of **Sāttvikābhinaya**.
- **Connection with the Divine**: The aim of Odissi is not just to perform but to create a spiritual connection with the audience. The dancer embodies the emotions of the character being portrayed, allowing the audience to experience the narrative on a deeper emotional level.

Odissi, with its rich tapestry of movements, emotions, and spirituality, serves as a profound form of expression that resonates deeply with audiences. By integrating the four types of Abhinaya—**Āṅgikābhinaya**, **Vācikābhinaya**, **Āhāryābhinaya**, and **Sāttvikābhinaya**—Odissi dancers bring forth a holistic performance that is both visually stunning and emotionally engaging. This dance form not only showcases the technical prowess of the dancer but also reflects the rich cultural heritage of India, inviting audiences into a world of divine beauty and devotion.

2. Indian Theater Traditions

Traditional Indian theater, such as *Koodiyattam, Yakshagana,* and *Kathakali,* combines dance, music, and acting to create a multi-sensory experience. Sanskrit drama, which flourished between the 3rd and 10th centuries CE, is characterized by its focus on spiritual and moral themes. The *Natya Shastra* prescribes elaborate guidelines for the staging of plays, including the use of symbolic gestures, music, and poetry to convey complex emotions and philosophical ideas.

2.1 Kathakali: Dramatic Expression and Epic Storytelling

Kathakali, a highly dramatic and elaborate dance-drama from Kerala, is known for its bold makeup, exaggerated facial expressions, and retelling of episodes from the **Mahābhārata** and **Rāmāyaṇa**.

Kathakali

- **Āṅgikābhinaya:** Kathakali is characterized by bold, dramatic movements, especially in the hands and facial muscles. Dancers use **Mudras** (hand gestures) to communicate, and the expressions around the eyes are incredibly intricate. The body movements are highly choreographed and slow, following the rhythms of the accompanying music.
- **Vācikābhinaya:** Although Kathakali dancers do not speak, the performance is accompanied by live singing in **Malayalam** or Sanskrit, with a focus on rhythmic drumming using instruments like the **chenda** and **maddalam.** The singers narrate the epic tales while the dancers express the emotions physically.
- **Āhāryābhinaya:** Kathakali costumes are elaborate and vibrant, with exaggerated facial makeup to distinguish

characters (green for gods and heroes, red for demons). The costumes include large skirts, headdresses, and ornamental jewelry, making the dancers appear larger than life.

- **Sāttvikābhinaya**: Kathakali requires an intense internalization of emotions. The dancer must embody divine or demonic characters, showcasing extreme emotions like rage, heroism, or sorrow. The audience must feel the emotions through the dancer's internal energy, conveyed through their eyes and expressions.

2.2 Koodiyattam: The Ancient Sanskrit Drama of Kerala

Koodiyattam is a 2,000-year-old Sanskrit theater tradition from Kerala. It is one of the oldest forms of theater in India, performed inside temples, and focuses on slow, deliberate storytelling with complex layers of meaning.

Koodiyattam

- **Āṅgikābhinaya:** Koodiyattam performers use extremely controlled and precise body movements. Each gesture is symbolic, with **Mudras** (hand gestures) being central to the narration. The pace of Koodiyattam is intentionally slow, allowing for detailed storytelling.
- **Vācikābhinaya:** The spoken part is often in **Sanskrit** or **Prakrit**, with chants or verses used to enhance the spiritual aspect of the performance. The narrative is both sung and spoken, emphasizing the text's religious and philosophical undertones.
- **Āhāryābhinaya:** The makeup and costumes are intricate and have deep symbolic meanings. Like Kathakali, Koodiyattam costumes feature elaborate headgear, jewelry, and face paint that represent the characters' nature.
- **Sāttvikābhinaya:** Internal emotions are at the core of Koodiyattam, with the performer's emotional depth playing a crucial role. The dancer conveys profound spiritual and emotional states through minimal, subtle facial movements and eye gestures.

2.3 Yakshagāna: The Dance-Drama Tradition of Karnataka

Yakshagāna is a traditional dance-drama form originating from the coastal regions of Karnataka, India. It is characterized by its vibrant performances that blend dance, music, dialogue, and elaborate costumes, often depicting themes from Hindu epics like the **Mahābhārata** and **Rāmāyaṇa**. Yakshagāna translates to "the song of the celestial beings," reflecting its mythological roots.

Yakshagāna

Āṅgikābhinaya in Yakshagāna encompasses the intricate movements and gestures of the performers.

- **Dance Movements**: The dance style is energetic and expressive, featuring stylized movements that are both rhythmic and dramatic. Performers often engage in dynamic footwork and quick turns, embodying the characters they portray. The postures reflect a strong connection to the storytelling, with each movement designed to convey specific emotions and narratives.
- **Facial Expressions**: Facial expressions play a crucial role in Yakshagāna, as they help convey the inner emotions of the characters. Performers utilize exaggerated expressions to evoke emotions such as anger, joy, and sorrow, allowing the audience to connect with the story being told.

Vācikābhinaya in Yakshagāna integrates music, dialogue, and singing, creating a rich auditory experience.

- **Musical Accompaniment**: The performances are accompanied by traditional instruments, such as the **maddale** (a type of drum), **harmonium**, and **flute**, providing a rhythmic and melodic backdrop. The music is lively and sets the mood for the performance, often changing according to the narrative's emotional tone.
- **Dialogue and Lyrics**: The performers recite dialogues in **Kannada** or sometimes in a mix of **Tulu** and other regional languages. The dialogue is often poetic and filled with metaphors, contributing to the overall theatrical experience. The interplay of spoken dialogue and singing enriches the narrative, with performers often improvising based on audience reactions.

Āhāryābhinaya in Yakshagāna is notable for its elaborate costumes and striking makeup.

- **Costumes**: The costumes are colorful and ornate, often made of rich fabrics adorned with intricate patterns. Male characters typically wear **dhoti** (a traditional garment) and a **shawl**, while female characters don **sarees** embellished with jewelry and ornamental designs that reflect their character's status.
- **Makeup**: The makeup in Yakshagāna is striking and serves to enhance the performers' expressions. The face is often painted in vibrant colors, with specific patterns representing different characters. For example, **demon characters** might have red or black faces, while **gods and heroes** are depicted with more benign colors.

Sāttvikābhinaya in Yakshagāna focuses on the internal emotional expression of the performers.

- **Emotional Engagement**: The actors must internalize the emotions of the characters they portray, effectively bringing the stories to life through their expressions. This internalization is reflected in the nuances of their facial expressions and body language, which resonate with the audience.
- **Spiritual Connection**: Yakshagāna performances often aim to create a spiritual atmosphere, inviting the audience to reflect on the themes of love, duty, and morality inherent in the narratives. The performers' ability to convey complex emotions helps to establish a connection between the characters and the audience, allowing them to feel the weight of the story's themes.

Yakshagāna is a vibrant and dynamic dance-drama tradition that combines the elements of Āṅgikābhinaya, Vācikābhinaya, Āhāryābhinaya, and Sāttvikābhinaya to create a rich theatrical experience. Through its energetic performances, vivid storytelling, and emotive expressions, Yakshagāna not only entertains but also imparts moral and spiritual lessons drawn from ancient epics. This unique art form continues to thrive in Karnataka, showcasing the region's cultural heritage and artistic diversity.

3.The Role of Saḥrudaya in Indian Theatrical Tradition

In Indian theater, the audience's participation is crucial. The concept of *Sahridaya*—a shared understanding or emotional connection between the performer and the audience—enhances the collective experience. The performers rely on the audience's reactions to gauge the effectiveness of their portrayal of *Rasa*.

Saḥrudaya, a term derived from the Sanskrit words **"Saha"** (together) and **"Hridaya"** (heart), refers to the concept of a sensitive audience member who can empathize with the emotions and experiences presented in a performance. In the context of Indian theatrical traditions, the role of saḥrudaya is crucial, as it embodies the interactive and participatory nature of performance, fostering a deeper emotional connection between the performers and the audience. The concept of saḥrudaya has its roots in ancient Indian aesthetics and drama, particularly in texts such as **Natyashastra** by Bharata Muni. Bharata emphasizes that the effectiveness of performance is greatly enhanced when the audience is capable of feeling and understanding the emotions conveyed on stage.

- **Aesthetic Experience**: According to the Natyashastra, the ideal spectator is one who can appreciate the **rasa** (flavor or aesthetic experience) of a performance. The notion of rasa is integral to Indian aesthetics and is closely tied to the saḥrudaya. A true saḥrudaya experiences the rasa through their engagement with the emotional landscape of the narrative.

3.1. Empathy and Emotional Resonance

Sahrudaya is pivotal in the experience of empathy during theatrical performances.

Identification with Characters: A saḥrudaya identifies with the characters on stage, feeling their joys, sorrows, and struggles. This identification fosters a shared emotional journey, allowing the audience to engage with the narrative on a profound level. The audience's emotional responses often reflect the performers' abilities to evoke strong feelings, making the performance a collaborative experience.

Cultivation of Emotional Depth: Sahrudayas are expected to possess a level of emotional intelligence that allows them to connect with the subtleties of the performance. Their responses enhance the emotional depth of the experience, encouraging performers to convey a wider range of emotions and narratives.

3.2. Role in Different Theatrical Forms

The role of sahrudaya varies across different Indian theatrical traditions, each emphasizing its unique connection with the audience.

- Classical Dance and Drama: In forms such as Kathakali, Bharatanatyam, and Koodiyattam, the sahrudaya plays a crucial role in interpreting the nuanced gestures, expressions, and movements of the performers. These dance forms rely heavily on the audience's ability to perceive and resonate with the emotions conveyed through **Abhinaya** (expressive art), where a sahrudaya's understanding can enhance the performance's impact.

- Folk Theatre: In folk traditions like Yakshagāna or Nukkad Natak, the audience's active participation is often encouraged. The sahrudaya engages not just through observation but also through interaction, allowing for a dynamic exchange between performers and spectators. This interactive nature emphasizes the communal aspect of these performances, making the audience an integral part of the theatrical experience.

- Modern Indian Theatre: In contemporary Indian theatre, the role of sahrudaya remains relevant, as plays often tackle complex social issues. The audience's ability to empathize with the characters and themes presented can influence the overall reception and impact of the performance, driving home the message intended by the playwright.

3.3. Cultural Significance

The concept of sahrudaya holds significant cultural implications in the context of Indian theater.

- **Promotion of Shared Values**: Sahrudaya contribute to the reinforcement of cultural values and social norms through their engagement with theatrical narratives. By resonating with the characters' experiences, audiences are encouraged to reflect on their values and beliefs, creating a sense of communal identity.
- **Preservation of Tradition**: As empathetic spectators, sahrudaya play a key role in preserving and transmitting cultural traditions. Their active participation and emotional responses help maintain the relevance of traditional performances, ensuring that the stories and teachings continue to resonate with contemporary audiences.

The role of sahrudaya in Indian theatrical tradition is fundamental to the success and impact of performances. As sensitive audience members, sahrudaya fosters a profound emotional connection with the narratives and characters on stage. Their ability to empathize enhances the aesthetic experience of rasa, promoting a shared journey of emotions between performers and spectators. This symbiotic relationship not only enriches the theatrical experience but also preserves and perpetuates cultural values, making sahrudaya an indispensable element of Indian theatrical tradition.

Performance in African Culture

Performance in African cultures is deeply embedded in the fabric of social and spiritual life. African performance traditions, including music, dance, storytelling, and ritual, serve as a means of communication, education, and community bonding. African performances are often characterized by their interactive nature, with a strong emphasis on audience participation. The line between performer and spectator is fluid, creating a communal experience that is both inclusive and immersive.

Performance in African culture is an integral, vibrant, and multifaceted aspect of daily life that extends beyond entertainment to encapsulate cultural, religious, political, and social dimensions. The term "performance" in the African context refers to a wide variety of artistic expressions, including music, dance, theater, oral storytelling, rituals, and other forms of communal activities. These performances are deeply rooted in African traditions, where art and life are interconnected, and the act of performance serves as a means of communicating cultural values, beliefs, historical narratives, and social commentary.

Unlike the Western notion of performance as a distinct or isolated art form, African perpformance is holistic and participatory. It transcends the boundaries between performer and audience, with everyone actively contributing to the event. Whether it be a village ceremony, a festival, a rite of passage, or a simple gathering, performances are moments where the community comes together to share stories, celebrate, mourn, and educate.

1.

African Dance: A Detailed Exploration

African dance is a multifaceted and deeply ingrained aspect of the cultural, social, and spiritual life of African communities. It is not just a form of artistic expression but also a way of communicating and reinforcing community values, celebrating rites of passage, and maintaining social order. African dance varies widely across the continent, reflecting the diversity of its people, but it is unified by its connection to rhythm, music, and movement, as well as its deep ties to the community.

1.1. Historical and Cultural Context of African Dance

Dance in Africa is as ancient as the continent itself, with evidence of its existence dating back thousands of years. African dance has traditionally been passed down orally through generations, with each dance carrying a specific meaning and purpose. Historically, African dance has been intertwined with the daily life of African communities, used to celebrate births, marriages, harvests, funerals, and other important milestones.

Each region, ethnic group, and community in Africa has its own unique dance traditions, influenced by their environment, social structures, and spiritual beliefs. For instance, the dances of the Maasai in East Africa are distinct from the masked dances of the Dogon in West Africa, yet both serve similar purposes: reinforcing community ties, celebrating life, and honoring ancestors.

1.2. Forms and Styles of African Dance

African dance is characterized by its diversity, with numerous forms and styles across the continent. These can be broadly categorized based on geographical regions and functions:

a. West African Dance

West African dance is perhaps the most globally recognized form of African dance, with its vibrant rhythms and energetic movements. Countries like Senegal, Ghana, Nigeria, and Guinea are known for their intricate dance styles, often accompanied by drums, especially the djembe.

- **Kpanlogo (Ghana):** Originating among the Ga people, this dance is a mix of traditional and modern influences, often performed during festivals and celebrations. It involves energetic footwork and expressive arm movements.
- **Sabar (Senegal):** Performed by the Wolof people, the Sabar dance is known for its fast-paced drumming and dynamic movements, often performed during weddings and naming ceremonies.

Sabar (Senegal)

- **Yankadi-Macru (Guinea):** A two-part dance that begins slowly and becomes faster, reflecting the transition from courtship (Yankadi) to celebration (Macru).

b. East African Dance

East African dance traditions are more fluid and often connected to pastoralist cultures, where dance serves as a social activity during communal events like weddings or cattle celebrations.

- **Adumu (Maasai):** Also known as the "jumping dance," this traditional dance of the Maasai men involves participants jumping as high as possible while maintaining a rhythmic chant. It is performed as part of the initiation into adulthood.

Adumu (Maasai)

- **Ngoma (Tanzania, Uganda, Kenya):** The Swahili word for "drum," Ngoma also refers to the dance that accompanies the drum. Ngoma dances are usually performed during ceremonies and can involve complex footwork, hand clapping, and syncopated rhythms.

c. Central and Southern African Dance

In Central and Southern Africa, dance is often tied to rituals, agricultural festivals, and rites of passage, with an emphasis on community participation and symbolism.

- **Mbakumba (Zimbabwe):** This dance is associated with the Shona people and is performed during harvest celebrations. The dance involves intricate foot movements and symbolic gestures to honor the earth's fertility.
- **Makishi (Zambia):** This masked dance of the Lunda and Luvale people is performed during the mukanda, an initiation ceremony for boys transitioning into adulthood. The performers represent ancestral spirits, and the dance connects the living with their ancestors.

d. North African Dance

North African dance traditions are influenced by Arab, Berber, and Mediterranean cultures, blending African rhythm with Middle Eastern aesthetics.

- **Gnawa (Morocco):** The Gnawa people perform a trance-like dance accompanied by hypnotic music, drums, and chants. This dance is rooted in the healing rituals of Sufi mysticism, aimed at achieving spiritual transcendence.

Gnawa (Morocco)

1.3. Cultural Significance of African Dance

African dance is inextricably linked to the cultural and spiritual life of African communities. It is used to mark important events in the life cycle of an individual or community, such as:

- **Rites of Passage:** Many African dances are performed during rites of passage, including birth, puberty, marriage, and death. These dances serve as a way to honor the individual and integrate them into their community or spiritual realm. For example, the *Mukanda* initiation dance in Zambia is a critical element in transitioning boys into manhood.
- **Religious and Spiritual Practices:** African dance often has a spiritual or religious dimension, connecting the physical world with the ancestral or divine realm. In many cultures, dances are performed as offerings to gods, spirits, or ancestors to seek blessings, protection, or healing. The *Egungun* masquerade dance of the

Yoruba people in Nigeria, for example, honors ancestors by invoking their presence through intricate masked dances.

- **Community and Social Cohesion**: Dance in Africa often serves to reinforce social cohesion, as it is performed in communal settings and encourages participation. It is a way for communities to bond, celebrate shared experiences, and resolve conflicts. Dance becomes a medium through which social structures and hierarchies are maintained, as well as a tool for communication.

- **Resistance and Protest**: Throughout history, African dance has also been a form of resistance and protest, particularly during the colonial and post-colonial periods. In some contexts, dance became a way to preserve cultural identity in the face of oppression. In modern times, African dance forms have been used to highlight political issues, such as the *Toyi-Toyi* dance in South Africa, which became a powerful symbol of resistance during the apartheid era.

1.4. Key Elements of African Dance

African dance is often characterized by several key elements, which distinguish it from Western dance traditions:

- **Polyrhythm**: African dances are deeply rhythmic, often involving polyrhythms, where dancers move to multiple rhythms at the same time. This creates a complex and dynamic interaction between the music and movement.

- **Call-and-Response**: A fundamental feature of many African performances, call-and-response is present in African dance as well, where the dancer or lead drummer will initiate a movement or rhythm, and the community responds. This form highlights the participatory nature of African dance.

- **Isolation of Body Parts**: African dance frequently involves the isolation of different body parts, with dancers moving their arms, legs, hips, and torso independently in intricate patterns. This emphasizes control and coordination, allowing dancers to express complex emotions and ideas through their movements.
- **Grounded Movements**: African dances are generally earthbound, with dancers moving close to the ground, symbolizing their connection to the earth and their ancestors. This grounded style contrasts with the more elevated or "balletic" movements seen in Western dance.

1.5. Evolution and Influence of African Dance in Modern Times

In contemporary times, African dance continues to evolve, blending traditional elements with modern influences. African dances have had a profound impact on global dance culture, particularly through the African diaspora. The transatlantic slave trade spread African dance traditions to the Americas, where they contributed to the development of new dance forms such as jazz, samba, capoeira, and hip-hop.

Modern African dance is also flourishing within Africa itself, where traditional dances are being revitalized and adapted to address contemporary social and political issues. Many African dancers and choreographers are blending traditional movements with modern dance techniques to create innovative and expressive art forms that resonate with global audiences. For example, artists such as Germaine Acogny from Senegal, widely regarded as the "mother of contemporary African dance," have pioneered new dance forms that honor African traditions while pushing the boundaries of performance. African dance continues to be a powerful tool for storytelling, social activism, and the preservation of cultural heritage.

African dance is a living, breathing art form that reflects the soul of Africa. It is a powerful means of cultural expression, deeply connected to the rhythms of daily life, the spiritual world, and the communal ethos of African societies. African dance, in all its diversity, continues to evolve and inspire, playing a vital role in preserving the continent's rich cultural heritage while shaping global dance traditions. Whether performed in a village square, a modern stage, or as part of a protest, African dance remains a testament to the resilience, creativity, and communal spirit of African peoples.

2. African Music: A Detailed Exploration

African music, much like African dance, is a vital expression of cultural identity, social cohesion, and spiritual beliefs across the continent. It serves as a medium for communication, celebration, and education. The music of Africa is incredibly diverse, reflecting the continent's vast ethnic, linguistic, and cultural diversity. Traditional African music is typically functional, meaning it is closely tied to various aspects of life, including rituals, work, entertainment, and storytelling.

Dance and music are inseparable in African cultural practices. African dances are often accompanied by live music, featuring traditional instruments such as drums, flutes, and stringed instruments. These performances are not only artistic expressions but also carry social, political, and spiritual significance. They are performed at various occasions, such as festivals, weddings, funerals, and rites of passage, serving as a medium for storytelling, celebration, mourning, and spiritual connection.

In many African cultures, the drum is considered a sacred instrument, symbolizing the heartbeat of the community. The rhythm of the drum is believed to have the power to invoke spiritual forces, communicate with ancestors, and induce trance states. As Kwabena Nketia notes: "The drum is not just a musical instrument; it is a voice, a medium for spiritual and communal expression" (Nketia, *African Music in Ghana*, p. 102). The participatory nature of African dance and music rituals is central to their aesthetic impact. The audience often joins in the performance, clapping, singing, or dancing along, creating a collective emotional and spiritual experience. This participation blurs the boundaries between performer and spectator, emphasizing the communal nature of African aesthetic practices.

2.1. Historical and Cultural Context of African Music

African music is as ancient as the continent itself, deeply intertwined with the social, spiritual, and political lives of African people. It is integral to community events, religious ceremonies, and daily activities. Traditionally, African music was not recorded but passed down orally, making it a dynamic and ever-evolving art form.

Music in African societies is rarely performed in isolation. It is almost always connected to dance, ritual, or another form of communal activity. Historically, African music was used to celebrate life events such as births, weddings, and harvests, as well as to honor ancestors and deities.

Across Africa, different regions and ethnic groups have developed distinct musical traditions. For instance, the polyphonic vocal music of the Pygmy groups in Central Africa contrasts with the complex drumming rhythms of West Africa or the lyre and harp music of East Africa. These regional distinctions contribute to the rich mosaic of African musical styles.

2.2. Instruments of African Music

African music is known for its vast array of musical instruments, many of which are handcrafted using local materials such as wood, animal skins, and gourds. The instruments used in African music are deeply symbolic and often reflect the cultural and spiritual significance of the music being played.

a. Percussion Instruments

Percussion is at the heart of African music, and drums are perhaps the most iconic of African musical instruments. They serve not only as musical instruments but also as tools for communication.

- **Djembe (West Africa):** The djembe is one of the most popular and recognizable drums in African music. It is played with bare hands and produces a wide range of tones, from deep bass to sharp, high-pitched notes. The djembe is central to many West African musical traditions and is often used in communal events, celebrations, and rituals.
- **Talking Drum (West Africa):** Known as the *donno* in Ghana and *dùndún* in Nigeria, the talking drum is unique because it can mimic the tone and rhythm of human speech. It is used to send messages across distances and to accompany songs and dances.

- **Dundun (Mali, Guinea, Nigeria)**: A cylindrical drum played with sticks, the dundun is used in ensembles with other drums to create polyrhythmic music. It is particularly important in the griot traditions of West Africa, where it accompanies praise songs and historical epics.
- **Balafon (West Africa)**: A type of wooden xylophone, the balafon is common in West African music. It is made from wooden slats that are struck with mallets and is often used in storytelling and ceremonial music.

b. String Instruments

String instruments are also prominent in African music, varying from simple plucked instruments to complex multi-stringed harps.

- **Kora (West Africa)**: A 21-stringed harp-lute used by the Mandinka people, the kora is traditionally played by *griots* or *jeli* (oral historians). Its sound is delicate and melodic, often used to accompany epic storytelling or praise singing.
- **Ngoni (Mali)**: The ngoni is a small string instrument, considered one of the oldest in West Africa. It has been the ancestor to many modern stringed instruments, including the banjo, and is traditionally used by *griots* in Mali.
- **Kissar (Nubia/Egypt)**: This ancient lyre has been used for centuries in Northeast Africa and was played in both religious and secular contexts. It has five strings and is associated with the Coptic church in Ethiopia.

c. Wind Instruments

Wind instruments in African music are often made from local materials such as wood, bamboo, or animal horns, and they produce a variety of sounds used in different musical contexts.

- **Vuvuzela (Southern Africa)**: A long, plastic horn that produces a loud monotone, the vuvuzela gained international attention during the 2010 FIFA World Cup in South Africa. Historically, wind instruments like animal horns or flutes served as ceremonial instruments in many African societies.
- **Algaita (Nigeria)**: A double-reed wind instrument, similar to an oboe, the algaita is used in Hausa music for royal ceremonies and celebrations.

d. Idiophones

Idiophones are instruments that produce sound from the material itself without needing strings or a membrane. African idiophones include a range of bells, rattles, and other percussion instruments.

- **Mbira (Zimbabwe)**: Also known as the thumb piano, the mbira consists of metal keys attached to a wooden board and is played by plucking the keys with the thumbs. It is used in spiritual ceremonies and for storytelling among the Shona people of Zimbabwe.
- **Shekere (West Africa)**: A gourd covered with a net of beads, the shekere is a rattle that is shaken or struck to create a rhythmic accompaniment for dances and songs.

2.3. Rhythm and Polyrhythm in African Music

One of the defining features of African music is its use of rhythm, particularly polyrhythm, where multiple rhythms are played simultaneously. These complex rhythms are often created using various percussion instruments, each contributing a different rhythmic pattern. The resulting music is layered, dynamic, and highly expressive.

Polyrhythm is integral to African music because it reflects the communal nature of African society, where individuals contribute to the collective whole. In African music, different instruments, voices, or body movements may follow their own rhythmic patterns, but they all come together to create a cohesive and harmonious sound.

The structure of African music often involves cyclical patterns, where a rhythmic phrase or melody is repeated with slight variations over time. This creates a sense of continuity and allows for improvisation, making each performance unique.

2.4. Cultural Significance of African Music

African music serves various functions within the social, spiritual, and political life of African communities. It is not just a form of entertainment; it is a means of communication, a way to mark important life events, and a tool for social organization.

a. Religious and Spiritual Context

Music is a central component of many African religious practices. In African traditional religions, music is used to connect with the spiritual world, communicate with ancestors, and invoke deities. Songs and chants often accompany rituals, sacrifices, and prayers. For instance, in Yoruba religion, *bàtá* drumming is used to communicate with the orishas (deities).

In some cultures, music is believed to have healing properties. Specific rhythms, melodies, or songs are used in rituals to cure illness, ward off evil spirits, or bring about fertility. The healing power of music is deeply embedded in African belief systems, where sound is considered a vital force that can affect the physical and spiritual realms.

b. Social and Political Commentary

Throughout history, African music has been a tool for social and political expression. During the colonial period, African musicians used music to critique colonial rule and express resistance. Songs often contained hidden messages or symbolic meanings that conveyed defiance or hope for freedom.

In post-colonial Africa, music has continued to serve as a platform for addressing social issues such as corruption, inequality, and human rights abuses. Artists like Fela Kuti in Nigeria and Miriam Makeba in South Africa used their music to criticize oppressive regimes and advocate for social justice.

c. Rites of Passage and Ceremonies

African music plays an important role in rites of passage, such as birth, initiation, marriage, and death. Each life stage is accompanied by specific musical traditions, designed to honor the individual and reinforce their place within the community. For instance, in many cultures, drums and chants are used to accompany the transition from childhood to adulthood during initiation ceremonies.

Funeral music is also a significant tradition in many African societies. It serves to honor the deceased, guide their spirit into the afterlife, and comfort the bereaved. For example, the *dirge* in many West African cultures is a lamenting song performed to mourn the dead and celebrate their life.

5.5. Modern African Music and Global Influence

African music has undergone significant transformation in the modern era, blending traditional elements with contemporary genres to create new, hybrid forms. The global influence of African music can be seen in various genres such as jazz, blues, salsa, samba, reggae, and hip-hop, which all have roots in African musical traditions.

a. Afrobeat and Highlife

In West Africa, the fusion of traditional rhythms with Western instruments led to the development of genres like *Highlife* and *Afrobeat*. Fela Kuti, a pioneer of Afrobeat, blended traditional Yoruba music with jazz and funk, creating a sound that was both political and danceable. Highlife, which originated in Ghana, combines traditional Akan music with Western brass instruments and has become a popular genre throughout West Africa. Its upbeat rhythms and danceable melodies reflect the blending of African and Western musical traditions.

b. African Hip-Hop and Pop

In the contemporary African music scene, hip-hop and pop music have become increasingly popular, particularly among younger generations. African hip-hop often incorporates traditional beats and languages, while addressing modern social issues such as poverty, inequality, and corruption.

c. Contemporary African Music

In recent years, contemporary African musicians have gained international recognition, with genres like Afrobeats and hip-hop becoming prominent on the global stage. Artists such as Burna Boy, Wizkid, and Angelique Kidjo are celebrated for their innovative approaches, blending traditional African sounds with modern influences to create music that resonates with diverse audiences.

- **Music Festivals and Platforms**: Festivals such as the Harare International Festival of the Arts (HIFA) in

Zimbabwe and the Festival au Désert in Mali celebrate African music, providing platforms for artists to showcase their work and connect with global audiences.

d. Digital Revolution

The advent of digital technology has transformed the way African music is produced, distributed, and consumed. Social media platforms, streaming services, and music videos have enabled artists to reach global audiences and collaborate across borders, creating new opportunities for exposure and innovation.

African music is a vibrant and essential aspect of the continent's cultural heritage, reflecting the diverse histories, traditions, and social realities of its people. Through its rhythms, melodies, and communal spirit, African music serves as a powerful means of expression, storytelling, and social commentary.

Storytelling and Oral Traditions

Storytelling is a fundamental aspect of African performance traditions. Oral narratives, passed down through generations, play a crucial role in preserving history, culture, and moral values. Storytellers, known as *griots* in West African cultures, are revered as custodians of cultural knowledge and history. They use a combination of speech, song, and gesture to engage their audience, making storytelling a performative and interactive art form.

African storytelling often involves call-and-response techniques, where the audience actively participates by responding to the storyteller's prompts, thereby becoming co-creators of the narrative. This interactive mode of storytelling reinforces communal bonds and ensures the transmission of cultural knowledge and values. Ama Ata Aidoo captures the essence of this oral tradition in her novel *The Dilemma of a Ghost*:

"The stories are alive. They move and breathe, and we, their listeners, give them life" (Aidoo, *The Dilemma of a Ghost*, p. 67).

The performative nature of African storytelling enhances its aesthetic appeal, making it not only a medium of communication but also a powerful tool for emotional and cultural expression.

The intersection of Indian and African emotional theories offers a rich tapestry of insights into how emotions are expressed, perceived, and culturally constructed through storytelling, folktales, folk songs, and aesthetic theories such as the Indian *Rasa* theory. Both traditions emphasize the communal and relational aspects of emotions, viewing them not just as individual experiences but as integral to the fabric of society, culture, and spirituality. This exploration will highlight how these emotional theories converge and diverge through various cultural expressions.

Storytelling and Emotional Expression

Storytelling is a fundamental aspect of both Indian and African cultures, serving as a means to transmit knowledge, values, and emotional experiences across generations. In both traditions, stories are often communal events, bringing together audiences to engage emotionally with the narrative.

In Indian tradition, storytelling is deeply intertwined with *Rasa* theory, which articulates the emotional responses evoked by art. The *Rasa* concept posits that emotions such as love, fear, and joy are not merely felt but are aesthetic experiences that can be cultivated and appreciated through performance and narrative. The *Nāṭyaśāstra*, an ancient Indian treatise on performing arts, emphasizes that the effective portrayal of *Rasa* can transport the audience into an emotional realm, creating a shared experience that resonates within the community. Storytellers, or *kathakars*, utilize various techniques to evoke these emotions, often weaving in elements of drama, music, and dance to enhance the emotional impact.

Similarly, in African traditions, storytelling is a communal practice that serves to reinforce social bonds and shared cultural identity. African folktales often feature trickster characters, moral lessons, and communal themes that resonate with listeners. These stories are typically performed by griots or oral historians who engage their audience through lively performances that invoke laughter, sorrow, or reflection. The emotional responses elicited through these narratives are rooted in the cultural context, often emphasizing communal values, ancestral connections, and the human experience. Just as in Indian storytelling, the African narrative tradition invites listeners to connect emotionally with the characters and themes, fostering a sense of belonging and shared identity.

Folktales and Collective Emotions

Folktales in both Indian and African cultures serve as vehicles for conveying collective emotions and shared values. These narratives often encapsulate the fears, hopes, and aspirations of the community, providing insight into their emotional landscape.

In Indian folklore, tales often explore themes of duty (*dharma*), love (*prema*), and moral dilemmas, resonating with the emotional experiences of individuals within a societal framework. For instance, the tale of Savitri and Satyavan, which narrates a woman's unwavering love and determination to bring her husband back from the clutches of death, evokes *śṛngāra* (the emotion of love) and *karuṇā* (the emotion of compassion). Such stories serve not only to entertain but also to reinforce social norms and emotional ideals within the community, illustrating how personal emotions are interwoven with collective narratives.

In African traditions, folktales often reflect the community's relationship with nature, ancestors, and the spirit world. The character of Anansi, the spider trickster in West African folklore, embodies cleverness and resilience, resonating with themes of survival and ingenuity. These tales often invoke emotional responses tied to cultural values, community resilience, and the struggle against adversity. Through the lens of emotional theory, African folktales illuminate how collective experiences of joy, sorrow, and moral complexity shape community identity.

Both traditions recognize the importance of collective memory and emotional resonance in shaping cultural identity. Folktales provide a shared narrative framework through which individuals can explore their emotions while reaffirming their ties to their cultural heritage.

Folk Songs and Emotional Connectivity

Folk songs serve as another powerful medium for expressing and experiencing emotions within both Indian and African cultures. These songs encapsulate the collective sentiments of the community, conveying feelings of love, loss, joy, and resistance.

In India, folk songs often reflect regional dialects, traditions, and the emotional landscape of everyday life. Songs accompanying agricultural practices, festivals, and rituals evoke a sense of belonging and shared identity. The *Rasa* theory informs the understanding of these folk songs, as they evoke specific emotions through their melodies, rhythms, and lyrics. For example, the songs sung during the harvest festival (*Pongal* or *Makar Sankranti*) not only celebrate agricultural abundance but also evoke feelings of gratitude, joy, and communal harmony. The emotional impact of these songs is heightened by their performance context, as they are often sung in groups, creating a collective emotional experience.

In African cultures, folk songs are integral to communal life, serving as a means of expressing historical narratives, social justice, and cultural identity. Songs such as those sung during work, rituals, or celebrations provide emotional catharsis and reinforce community ties. For instance, the powerful songs of resistance during the struggle against colonialism resonate with themes of hope, resilience, and solidarity. These songs create emotional connections that transcend individual experiences, inviting listeners to participate in a collective memory and shared struggle.

The communal nature of folk song performance in both traditions emphasizes the importance of emotional connectivity, fostering a sense of unity and belonging. In both Indian and African contexts, these songs are not just expressions of individual feelings but are part of a larger emotional narrative that reflects the community's identity and values.

Emotional Theories: Convergences and Divergences

The intersection of Indian and African emotional theories reveals both convergences and divergences in how emotions are understood and expressed through storytelling, folktales, and folk songs. Both traditions share a fundamental understanding that emotions are deeply embedded in cultural practices and communal experiences, emphasizing the relational nature of emotional expression.

The Indian *Rasa* theory provides a framework for understanding the aesthetic experience of emotions, suggesting that the evocation of specific feelings can be cultivated through artistic expression. This notion aligns with the African understanding of emotions as deeply connected to cultural practices, where storytelling and song serve as mediums for shared emotional experiences. Both traditions recognize the role of art in shaping emotional responses and fostering community ties.

However, there are also differences in how emotions are contextualized and articulated within each tradition. The Indian approach often emphasizes the categorization and analysis of emotions through *Rasa*, providing a systematic framework for understanding emotional experiences in literature and performance. In contrast, African emotional theories may be more fluid and less formally categorized, reflecting a diverse range of cultural practices and beliefs across various ethnic groups. The emphasis in African traditions on oral history and communal performance highlights the dynamic and evolving nature of emotional expression.

The intersection of Indian and African emotional theories through storytelling, folktales, and folk songs illuminates the profound connections between emotions, culture, and community. Both traditions offer rich insights into how emotions are expressed, experienced, and shared, emphasizing the importance of collective identity and relationality. Through these cultural expressions, individuals engage with their emotions, reinforcing their ties to their heritage while navigating the complexities of human experience.

As we explore the emotional landscapes of these diverse traditions, we are reminded of the universality of emotions and the ways in which storytelling and music serve as vital conduits for understanding and expressing our shared humanity. The convergence of Indian and African emotional theories not only enriches our understanding of these cultural traditions but also highlights the enduring power of art to evoke, reflect, and connect us to one another across time and space.

Comparative Analysis: Indian and African Performance Traditions

While Indian and African performance traditions are distinct in their forms and cultural contexts, they share common features that enhance the aesthetic experience and foster participation. Both traditions emphasize the performative and communal aspects of art, viewing performance as a means of connecting individuals to the spiritual realm.

1. The Role of the Audience

In both Indian and African performance traditions, the audience plays an active role in the aesthetic experience.

The concept of *Sahridaya* in Indian aesthetics, where the audience shares a deep emotional and spiritual connection with the performer, parallels the communal participation seen in African dance and storytelling. This shared experience enhances the emotional impact of the performance and fosters a sense of unity and belonging.

2. Spiritual and Emotional Engagement

Both Indian and African performances are often linked to spiritual and religious practices, serving as rituals that connect the physical and spiritual worlds. Indian classical dance and theater frequently portray stories from Hindu mythology, aiming to evoke *Rasa* and convey moral and spiritual lessons. Similarly, African performances often serve as conduits for spiritual communication, invoking ancestral spirits, and expressing communal values.

The emotional engagement in these performances is profound, as they address universal human experiences such as love, loss, joy, and suffering. This emotional resonance is achieved through the performative elements of music, dance, and expressive gestures, which are central to both Indian and African traditions.

3. Preservation of Cultural Heritage

Performance is a vital means of preserving and transmitting cultural heritage in both Indian and African societies. Through dance, music, and theater, cultural narratives, historical events, and moral values are passed down from generation to generation. This transmission ensures the continuity of cultural identity and serves as a form of resistance against cultural erasure.

In African societies, for example, oral traditions and performance play a crucial role in preserving history and cultural memory, particularly in the face of colonialism and globalization. Similarly, in India, classical dance and theater continue to thrive as living traditions that connect contemporary society with its rich cultural past.

Performance and participation are central to the aesthetic experience in both Indian and African cultures. Through dance, music, theater, and storytelling, these traditions create a space for communal engagement, emotional expression, and spiritual connection. The participatory nature of these performances not only enhances their aesthetic impact but also reinforces cultural values, social cohesion, and the continuity of cultural heritage. By examining the role of performance in these traditions, we gain a deeper understanding of the power of art to transcend boundaries, connect individuals, and evoke profound emotional and spiritual responses.

SYMBOLISM AND SPIRITUALITY

This chapter delves into the role of symbolism and spirituality in Indian and African narratives, highlighting how these two elements are deeply interwoven in the literary and cultural traditions of both regions. Symbolism, as a means of representing complex ideas through simple or familiar objects, and spirituality, as a connection to the divine or the sacred, play central roles in shaping the stories, values, and worldviews of Indian and African societies. By examining key literary texts, this chapter explores how symbolism serves as a conduit for spiritual meaning, linking the human and the divine in both Indian and African contexts.

1. Symbolism in Indian Culture and Narratives

Symbolism is a central and pervasive element in Indian culture and narratives, woven into religious, philosophical, and aesthetic traditions. The use of symbols allows complex ideas and values to be communicated with simplicity, depth, and universality. Indian literature, art, dance, and rituals are rich with symbols, often connecting the material and spiritual worlds. Below is a detailed exploration of symbolism in various aspects of Indian culture:

1.1 Symbolism in Hinduism and Indian Religions

Hinduism and other Indian religions like Buddhism and Jainism extensively use symbols to represent divine concepts, spiritual truths, and cosmic principles. These symbols serve as tools to convey abstract metaphysical ideas and facilitate deeper engagement with the sacred.

- **Om (Aum)**: Om is one of the most powerful symbols in Indian culture, representing the sound of the universe and the essence of ultimate reality (Brahman). It is used in meditation and rituals as a sonic representation of the divine.
- **Lotus (Padma)**: The lotus symbolizes purity, spiritual awakening, and the unfolding of consciousness. Though it grows in muddy water, it blossoms above the surface untouched by impurity, symbolizing the soul's journey toward enlightenment.
- **Trident (Trishula)**: Lord Shiva's trident symbolizes the three fundamental aspects of existence: creation, preservation, and destruction. It also signifies the conquering of time (past, present, future).
- **The Wheel (Dharma Chakra)**: This symbol is common in Buddhism and represents the path to enlightenment. The wheel's eight spokes represent the Eightfold Path, a fundamental Buddhist teaching.

- **Fire (Agni)**: Fire holds a dual symbolism of destruction and purification. In Vedic rituals, fire is a medium through which offerings are made to the gods. It is also a symbol of transformation, connecting the earthly and the divine.

1. **2. Symbolism in Indian Art and Architecture**

Indian art and architecture are rich with symbolic meanings. Temples, sculptures, and paintings depict gods, goddesses, and cosmological ideas with profound layers of symbolism.

- **Temple Architecture**: Indian temples are symbolically designed to represent the universe. The central dome or spire (Shikhara) is symbolic of Mount Meru, the axis mundi or the center of the universe in Hindu cosmology. The temple's layout mirrors the cosmos, guiding worshippers on a spiritual journey from the outer world to the inner sanctum (Garbhagriha).
- **Mandala Patterns**: Mandalas, geometric patterns, symbolize the universe and are used in religious rituals as visual aids to meditation. They represent the idea of wholeness and are employed in Hindu and Buddhist spiritual practices.
- **Mythical Creatures**: Indian art features creatures like the Naga (serpent), Garuda (eagle), and Yali (lion), which symbolize protection, divine power, and the balance between good and evil.

1. **3. Symbolism in Indian Dance and Drama**

Classical Indian dance forms such as Bharatanatyam, Kathak, and Odissi incorporate symbolic gestures (Mudras) and facial expressions (Abhinaya) to convey narratives from Indian epics and mythology.

- **Mudras (Hand Gestures)**: Each mudra in Indian dance represents a specific idea, feeling, or object. For example, the "Anjali" mudra symbolizes offering or prayer, while the "Hamsasya" mudra, resembling a swan, signifies beauty or purity.
- **Rasas**: In Indian drama (Natya Shastra), the concept of *Rasa* refers to emotional flavors that the audience experiences, such as Śṛṅgāra (love), Vīra (heroism), Karuṇa (sorrow), and Raudra (anger). Each emotion is represented through specific expressions and movements, adding a layer of symbolism to the performance.

1. **4. Symbolism in Indian Narratives and Epics**

Indian epics like the *Mahabharata* and *Ramayana*, along with Puranic stories, are replete with symbolic characters, events, and objects that offer moral, philosophical, and spiritual lessons.

- **Mahabharata**: The Kurukshetra war is symbolic of the eternal struggle between good and evil, dharma (righteousness) and adharma (unrighteousness). Characters like Arjuna symbolize the human soul in conflict, while Krishna represents divine guidance and the cosmic order.

- **Ramayana**: The narrative of Rama's exile, battle with Ravana, and return to Ayodhya is rich in symbolic meaning. Rama represents the ideal king, embodying dharma, while Ravana symbolizes ego and uncontrolled desires. Sita's trials and purity reflect the soul's journey through hardships and eventual redemption.
- **Churning of the Ocean (Samudra Manthan)**: This famous myth is a symbolic allegory of life's trials and the process of spiritual evolution. The churning of the ocean to extract amrita (nectar of immortality) symbolizes the spiritual seeker's struggles to overcome dualities and attain enlightenment.

1. **5. Symbolism in Indian Poetry and Literature**

Classical Indian poetry, especially in Sanskrit, Tamil, and other regional languages, uses highly symbolic language to explore themes of love, devotion, and the divine.

- **Metaphors of Nature**: Nature is often a mirror for human emotions. For example, the changing seasons in Kalidasa's poetry often symbolize the progression of emotions in love stories.
- **Symbolism in Bhakti Poetry**: Bhakti poets like Mirabai, Kabir, and Andal use symbols of everyday life (like the lover and the beloved) to convey the soul's longing for union with God. The language is simple yet filled with profound spiritual symbolism.
- **Alankara (Ornamentation)**: In classical Indian poetics, *Alankara* refers to rhetorical devices or embellishments, many of which are symbolic. Metaphors, similes, and allegories are used to evoke deeper meanings beyond

the literal.

1. **6. Symbolism in Indian Folklore and Mythology**

Indian folklore and mythological stories are rich in symbolic figures that convey moral lessons and cultural values.

- **Panchatantra and Jataka Tales**: Animals in these stories are symbolic of human virtues and vices. For instance, the lion might represent bravery, while the fox represents cunning.
- **Mythological Figures**: Figures like Lord Ganesha, with an elephant head and a human body, symbolize wisdom, intellect, and the removal of obstacles. Each of his attributes, such as his large ears and small mouth, carries symbolic meaning—listening more and speaking less, for instance.

In Indian culture and narratives, symbolism is not just a decorative device but a fundamental way of expressing complex philosophical, moral, and spiritual truths. From religion and art to literature and folklore, symbols provide a deeper understanding of the human experience, the nature of the cosmos, and the path to spiritual liberation. The intricate use of symbolism allows Indian narratives to communicate universal truths while remaining grounded in the cultural and spiritual ethos of the Indian subcontinent.

2. Spirituality in African Culture and Narratives

African spirituality, much like its Indian counterpart, is deeply connected to nature, community, and the cosmos. African narratives—both oral and written—are imbued with spiritual symbolism, often reflecting the interconnectedness of life, death, and the ancestors. In African literature, spiritual themes are often communicated through symbols that represent cultural beliefs, communal values, and the relationship between humans and the spiritual world.

Spirituality in African culture is deeply integrated into daily life, social structures, and narratives. African spiritual traditions are diverse, with each community having its own belief systems, but there are certain common threads, such as the belief in a supreme creator, the importance of ancestors, the cyclical nature of life and death, and the interconnection between the physical and spiritual worlds.

2.1. The Role of Ancestors in African Spirituality

Ancestors hold a significant place in African spiritual traditions. They are viewed as guardians, intermediaries between the living and the divine, and sources of wisdom and protection. Ancestors are deeply respected and honored through rituals, prayers, and offerings. In African narratives, the ancestral presence often reflects the continuity of life, offering moral guidance and upholding community values.

- **Intermediaries**: Ancestors act as mediators between the living and the spiritual realm. It is believed that they can influence the lives of their descendants by bringing blessings or causing harm if disrespected. Their role is crucial in maintaining the harmony of the family and community.
- **Guardians of Tradition**: Ancestors are seen as keepers of tradition and cultural identity. They are invoked to bless important rites of passage, such as births, weddings, and funerals, and are believed to oversee the moral and ethical behavior of the living.

- **Narratives and Ancestors**: In many African oral traditions, ancestors appear in folktales and epics as symbols of continuity, wisdom, and spiritual power. They are often invoked by characters who seek guidance or protection, reflecting their role as moral and spiritual exemplars.

Example: In the Yoruba tradition of West Africa, ancestors are revered as "Egungun." Ceremonies involving masked dancers representing ancestors are performed to honor and invoke their presence, ensuring the community's prosperity and spiritual well-being.

2.3. Spirituality in African Oral Tradition

African oral tradition serves as a powerful medium through which spirituality is expressed, preserved, and transmitted across generations. Spiritual themes such as the role of ancestors, the cycle of life and death, the relationship between humans and the divine, and the importance of community are intricately woven into stories, proverbs, songs, and rituals. Oral tradition not only functions as a repository of cultural memory but also as a living practice that reflects the dynamic nature of African spirituality.

2.3.1. Oral Tradition as a Spiritual Practice

Oral traditions are central to African spirituality because they act as vehicles through which spiritual wisdom and cultural values are passed on. These traditions often carry profound spiritual significance, serving as ways to communicate with the divine, remember the ancestors, and engage with the unseen forces of the universe.

- **Storytelling as a Spiritual Act**: Storytelling in many African cultures is more than entertainment; it is a sacred act that invokes the presence of ancestors and the divine. Storytellers, often called *griots* or *bards*, are seen as spiritual custodians who carry the responsibility of preserving cultural identity and transmitting moral and spiritual lessons. The act of storytelling can be a communal and ritualistic practice, invoking the spiritual energies of the past.

- **Proverbs and Spiritual Wisdom**: Proverbs are often regarded as repositories of spiritual and philosophical knowledge. They distill complex spiritual truths into simple, memorable phrases. For instance, many African proverbs emphasize the interconnectedness of life, community, and the spiritual world, reinforcing the belief that spiritual values guide daily life.

Example: The Akan proverb "The ancestors may be far away, but they are never absent" reflects the ever-present influence of the spiritual world, particularly ancestors, in everyday life.

2.4. Spiritual Themes in African Oral Narratives

African oral narratives, such as myths, folktales, and epics, are infused with spiritual themes that explore the relationship between humans, nature, the ancestors, and the divine. These narratives often reflect deep cosmological insights, explaining the origins of life, the nature of the divine, and the role of spiritual forces in shaping human destiny.

- **Creation Myths and Cosmology**: Many African cultures have creation myths that describe how the world and humans came into existence. These myths often feature a supreme deity, lesser gods, and ancestral spirits who shape the world. The spiritual significance of these myths lies in their ability to connect the listener with the divine origins of the world and the human race.

Example: The Dogon people of Mali have a rich cosmological tradition in which Amma, the supreme deity, creates the universe and all living beings. The myth explains the creation of the world through spiritual forces, emphasizing the role of divine will in the natural order.

- **Interaction with the Spirit World**: Many African folktales depict characters who interact with spirits, gods, or ancestors. These stories serve as allegories for human behavior and moral choices, illustrating the influence of spiritual forces in guiding individuals and communities. Characters often seek the help of spiritual beings to resolve conflicts, fulfill destinies, or restore harmony.

Example: In the Zulu tradition, the story of *Unkulunkulu* (the first being created by God) involves interactions between humans and spiritual forces, reflecting the belief in a divine power guiding human existence and the continuity of life through the ancestors.

- **Rites of Passage and Spiritual Narratives**: Oral narratives often accompany rites of passage, such as birth, initiation, marriage, and death. These stories serve to explain the spiritual significance of these life transitions, emphasizing the idea that humans are constantly moving between the physical and spiritual worlds.

Example: Initiation rites in many African societies are accompanied by stories that explain the spiritual transformation from childhood to adulthood. These narratives often emphasize the individual's new responsibilities toward the community and the spiritual world.

2.4 The Role of Ancestors in Oral Tradition

Ancestors play a central role in African oral traditions. They are believed to guide, protect, and communicate with the living through oral narratives. Stories involving ancestors serve as moral and spiritual lessons, reinforcing the idea that the wisdom of the past is essential for the present and future.

- **Ancestor Veneration through Oral Tradition**: Rituals involving the telling of ancestral stories keep the ancestors' presence alive within the community. These stories ensure that the values, traditions, and spiritual practices of the ancestors are maintained and honored. In some traditions, ancestors communicate through dreams or visions, which are interpreted and shared through oral narratives.

Example: In many African cultures, storytelling sessions begin with an invocation of the ancestors, acknowledging their spiritual presence and guidance during the telling of the story.

2.5. Life, Death, and the Afterlife in Oral Tradition

African oral traditions often express the cyclical nature of life, death, and the afterlife. Death is not seen as the end but as a transition to the spiritual realm, where the deceased become ancestors. This concept is frequently explored in oral narratives, which portray death as a spiritual journey rather than a final departure.

- **Cyclicality of Life and Death**: African oral stories emphasize the belief that life and death are interconnected. Life is seen as a temporary phase in the broader cycle of existence, with death leading to rebirth or entry into the ancestral world. These narratives teach that the living must honor the dead to maintain harmony between the physical and spiritual realms.

Example: In many African communities, the death of a revered elder is seen as their "becoming an ancestor," which is marked by storytelling rituals celebrating their life and contributions. These rituals often involve recounting their virtues and ensuring their spirit is honored.

- **The Journey of the Soul**: African oral traditions often feature the soul's journey after death. These narratives serve to comfort the living by affirming that the deceased have entered a spiritual world where they can continue to influence the living, offering protection and guidance.

2.6. Music, Dance, and Spirituality in Oral Tradition

Music and dance are integral to African oral traditions and often carry deep spiritual significance. They are used in rituals, ceremonies, and storytelling sessions to invoke spiritual powers, connect with ancestors, and facilitate communication with the divine.

- **Music as a Spiritual Medium**: In many African cultures, music is seen as a means of communication with the spiritual realm. Drums, in particular, are often considered sacred instruments that can summon spirits, ancestors, or gods during ceremonies. Songs and chants often carry spiritual messages, prayers, or invocations.

- **Dance as Spiritual Expression**: Dance is often a form of worship and a way to connect with spiritual forces. In many communities, specific dances are performed to honor the ancestors, invoke rain, ensure fertility, or mark important life transitions. The dance movements, rhythms, and costumes all carry symbolic meanings tied to spiritual beliefs.

Example: In the Shona culture of Zimbabwe, the *mbira* (thumb piano) is played during spiritual ceremonies to communicate with ancestral spirits. The music creates a trance-like state, allowing for communication between the spiritual and physical realms.

Spirituality in African oral tradition is not a separate entity from daily life but is deeply intertwined with how communities understand their place in the world, their history, and their relationship with the divine. Through storytelling, proverbs, music, dance, and rituals, African cultures preserve and express their spiritual values, emphasizing the interconnectedness of life, death, ancestors, and the cosmos. Oral tradition thus serves as both a spiritual and cultural bridge, connecting generations and ensuring the continuity of spiritual wisdom and practice.

Symbols of Life and Death

In African cultures, symbols of life and death are deeply rooted in spiritual and philosophical beliefs. Life and death are viewed as interconnected aspects of a continuous cycle, and many symbols serve to represent the transition between these states. These symbols often carry rich layers of meaning and are used in rituals, art, oral narratives, and daily practices to express spiritual truths and the interconnectedness of the physical and spiritual worlds.

1. Tree of Life

- Symbolism: The tree is a common symbol of life in many African cultures. It represents growth, nourishment, fertility, and the connection between heaven and earth. The roots of the tree, firmly grounded in the earth, symbolize human connection to ancestors and tradition, while the branches reaching upward symbolize spiritual growth and the link to the divine.
- Cultural Context: In many African cosmologies, trees are seen as sacred and are often associated with ancestors. Some African cultures believe that spirits reside in trees, making them a symbol of life, continuity, and the presence of the divine in nature.
- Example: In the Akan tradition of Ghana, the Baobab tree is often referred to as the "Tree of Life" and is associated with wisdom, longevity, and life-giving sustenance.

2. Water

- Symbolism: Water is a powerful symbol of life, fertility, and renewal in African spirituality. It represents the source of life, as it sustains all living things. However, water also has a dual nature, symbolizing death in certain contexts, as it can also be a destructive force (through floods or drowning) and a conduit between the physical and spiritual worlds.

- Ritual Significance: Water is used in many African spiritual rituals to purify, bless, or heal. It is often associated with the divine feminine, fertility, and the life-giving power of nature. In some cultures, water is seen as the gateway through which the dead pass into the ancestral realm.
- Example: In Yoruba culture, Oshun, the goddess of water, fertility, and love, is worshiped as the provider of life-giving waters. Rivers are considered sacred, and offerings are made to ensure fertility and prosperity.

3. The Serpent

- Symbolism: The serpent is a complex symbol in African culture, representing both life and death. It symbolizes fertility, regeneration, and transformation due to its ability to shed its skin, which mirrors the cycle of life, death, and rebirth. In some traditions, the serpent is also associated with the ancestors and the spiritual world.
- Duality of Life and Death: While the serpent is often seen as a symbol of life and renewal, it also represents death and the underworld in certain contexts. Its presence in African myths and rituals reflects the belief in the cyclical nature of existence, where life and death are intertwined.
- Example: Among the Dogon people of Mali, the serpent is considered a symbol of fertility and cosmic regeneration. The ancestral serpent *Lebe* is worshiped as the creator and sustainer of life, embodying both the creative and destructive forces of existence.

4. Masks

- Symbolism: Masks are significant in African rituals, particularly in relation to death and the afterlife. They are often used in funeral ceremonies and rites of passage to represent the presence of ancestors or spirits. Masks symbolize the transformation from the physical world to the spiritual realm and serve as intermediaries between the living and the dead.
- Ritual Function: In many African cultures, masks are worn by ritual dancers during funerals or ancestral celebrations to honor the deceased and guide their spirit into the afterlife. The mask wearer becomes a channel for the spirit, symbolizing the continuation of life through death and the ongoing influence of ancestors.
- Example: In the Igbo culture of Nigeria, the *Mmuo* masquerade involves dancers wearing elaborate masks that represent the spirits of the dead. These performances are part of funeral rites and are believed to help the deceased transition peacefully into the spiritual world.

5. The Circle

- Symbolism: The circle is a universal symbol of life, death, and continuity in African culture. It represents the cyclical nature of existence, where death is not the end but a part of the eternal cycle of life, death, and rebirth. The circle also symbolizes unity, completeness, and the interconnectedness of all beings—both living and spiritual.
- Cultural Context: Circles are often seen in African rituals, dances, and sacred symbols, representing the unity of the community, the connection between the physical and spiritual realms, and the endless cycle of

life and death.

- Example: In many African spiritual practices, dances are performed in a circular formation to symbolize the unity of the community and the ongoing cycle of life. These dances often take place during significant life events such as births, weddings, and funerals.

6. Calabash (Gourd)

- **Symbolism**: The calabash, or gourd, is often used as a symbol of both life and death in African culture. It is associated with fertility, sustenance, and life-giving power because it can hold water and food, essential for life. However, it is also used in funeral rituals, where it symbolizes death, transformation, and the passage into the spiritual world.
- **Duality of Life and Death**: In many African societies, the calabash is used in rituals that honor both the living and the dead. It represents the womb, the source of life, and the vessel that holds the soul as it transitions to the ancestral world.
- **Example**: In the Dinka culture of South Sudan, the calabash is a sacred object used in rituals related to fertility and funerals, symbolizing both the nurturing aspect of life and the transition to death.

7. Bones and Skulls

- **Symbolism**: Bones, particularly skulls, are potent symbols of death and the ancestral realm. They represent the presence of the ancestors and are often used in rituals to invoke their guidance and protection. Bones are seen as the remnants of life, holding the spiritual essence of the deceased.

- **Ritual Significance**: In many African spiritual practices, bones are used in divination and rituals to communicate with the ancestors or the spirit world. The bones of animals or humans may be used to predict the future or to seek ancestral wisdom, symbolizing the ongoing connection between life, death, and the spiritual realm.
- **Example**: Among the Zulu people of South Africa, bones are used in *sangoma* (traditional healer) divination practices. The throwing of bones is believed to provide insight into the spiritual forces influencing the lives of the living.

8. The Grave

- **Symbolism**: The grave in African cultures is not just a final resting place but a symbol of the transition from life to death and a connection point between the living and the ancestors. It is often seen as a sacred site where the dead can continue to influence the living. Graves are adorned with offerings, symbols of the deceased's life, and objects believed to aid in their journey to the spiritual world.
- **Cultural Practices**: Many African cultures engage in rituals around the grave, including periodic offerings, prayers, and ceremonies to ensure the deceased's peaceful rest and ongoing connection with the family. The grave symbolizes the portal between the earthly and spiritual realms.
- **Example**: In the Shona culture of Zimbabwe, after burial, families frequently visit graves to offer libations and communicate with their ancestors, ensuring that the spiritual connection remains strong.

Symbols of life and death in African culture are not just representations of abstract concepts but active participants in the spiritual and material worlds. They express the cyclical nature of existence, the interconnectedness between the living and the dead, and the continuous presence of spiritual forces in daily life. Whether through natural elements like water and trees or ritual objects like masks and bones, these symbols embody the African belief in the unity of life, death, and the afterlife, ensuring that the past, present, and future remain deeply connected.

3. Cross-Cultural Symbolism: Connecting Indian and African Narratives

Indian and African cultures, though geographically and historically distinct, share several underlying spiritual and symbolic connections, particularly through the sacredness of nature, the role of myth and archetypes, and the spirituality embedded in everyday life. These shared symbols and ideas reflect universal human experiences, but each culture also presents unique expressions of them within their respective narratives.

1. Sacredness of Nature

Nature holds a sacred place in both Indian and African spiritual systems. It is seen as a living force that embodies divine power, sustains life, and connects humans to the spiritual realm. Across Indian and African cultures, natural elements like trees, rivers, animals, and mountains are venerated for their sacredness and their roles as intermediaries between the physical and spiritual worlds.

- **Indian Context**: In Indian culture, nature is often viewed as a manifestation of the divine. Rivers, mountains, and trees are worshipped as deities or sacred entities. For example, the River Ganges is not only a water source but also personified as the goddess Ganga, representing purification and salvation. The Banyan tree, associated with immortality, is sacred and worshipped in many Indian traditions. Animals like cows, elephants, and snakes also carry religious significance, embodying divine attributes.

Example: The Ganges River in Hinduism is a symbol of purity and renewal. Its waters are believed to cleanse sins and offer spiritual liberation (moksha).

- **African Context**: Similarly, African spiritual traditions hold nature in high esteem, with many natural elements believed to house spirits or serve as dwellings for deities and ancestors. Rivers, forests, mountains, and animals are considered sacred, often playing a vital role in rituals and oral narratives. For example, in Yoruba spirituality, the goddess Oshun is associated with rivers, representing fertility, love, and abundance. The Baobab tree is revered in many African cultures as a symbol of life, wisdom, and resilience.

Example: The Baobab tree, known as the "Tree of Life," is significant in African traditions, symbolizing longevity, strength, and a deep connection to the earth.

- **Cross-Cultural Connection**: In both Indian and African narratives, nature is more than a backdrop; it is an active participant in the spiritual and material lives of the people. Rivers, trees, and animals embody divine presence, serving as bridges between the human and the cosmic order. In both cultures, the act of venerating nature highlights the importance of living in harmony with the environment, respecting its life-giving and spiritual forces.

2. The Role of Myth and Archetypes

Mythology and archetypes are foundational to the symbolic narratives in both Indian and African cultures. Myths explain the origins of the universe, human existence, and social values, while archetypal figures embody universal human traits and experiences, from heroism and sacrifice to wisdom and transformation.

- **Indian Context**: Indian mythology is vast and complex, populated by gods, goddesses, demons, and heroes who represent various cosmic forces and human virtues. Archetypes such as the hero (*Rama* in the *Ramayana*), the divine mother (*Parvati*, *Durga*), the trickster (*Krishna* in his playful aspects), and the wise sage (*Vyasa*, *Bhrigu*) are central to Indian narratives. These figures often undergo trials that reflect the moral and spiritual challenges of human life, offering guidance on dharma (righteousness) and karma (action and consequence).

Example: The archetype of the divine hero is seen in Rama, whose journey in the *Ramayana* embodies the triumph of good over evil, duty over personal desire, and the restoration of cosmic order (dharma).

- **African Context**: African myths and oral traditions also feature archetypal figures such as the hero, the trickster, the wise elder, and the mother figure. These figures often reflect communal values, such as bravery, wisdom, community cohesion, and respect for the natural and spiritual worlds. Trickster figures like Anansi (Ghana) or Eshu (Yoruba) play complex roles, representing chaos, change, and the balance between order and disorder.

Example: Anansi, the trickster spider from Akan folklore, symbolizes cleverness and wit, often using deception to outsmart others but also teaching important lessons about humility and justice.

- **Cross-Cultural Connection**: Both Indian and African narratives employ archetypes and myths to explore universal themes of human experience—struggle, growth, morality, and transformation. The hero's journey, the trickster's wisdom, and the mother's nurturing power are archetypes found in both cultures, illustrating shared human concerns and the use of symbolic figures to convey spiritual truths. These myths connect the physical and spiritual realms, providing insight into how human beings should live and interact with the universe.

3. Spirituality of the Everyday

In both Indian and African cultures, spirituality is not confined to religious ceremonies or sacred spaces but permeates everyday life. Daily actions, community interactions, and even mundane tasks are seen as imbued with spiritual significance. This idea of "living spirituality" connects people constantly to their ancestors, gods, and the natural world.

- **Indian Context**: In Indian culture, daily rituals such as lighting lamps, offering food to deities, and reciting prayers are integrated into the rhythm of everyday life. Activities like meditation, yoga, and chanting are spiritual practices meant to align the individual with the cosmos. The concept of *karma* teaches that every action has spiritual consequences, emphasizing the need for mindful and righteous living. Moreover, festivals like Diwali, Holi, and Pongal celebrate both life's spiritual and material aspects, blurring the lines between the sacred and the mundane.

Example: The practice of lighting a lamp at dawn and dusk in Indian households is not just a ritual; it symbolizes dispelling darkness (ignorance) and inviting divine light (knowledge and purity) into the home.

- **African Context**: In many African cultures, spirituality is similarly woven into the fabric of everyday life. Daily offerings to ancestors, prayers to spirits, and community gatherings are spiritual acts. Traditional healers, or shamans, use spiritual practices to address both physical and spiritual ailments, reflecting the belief that the two realms are interconnected. Community life itself is seen as a spiritual practice, where relationships, work, and social roles are understood within the context of larger spiritual and cosmic principles.

Example: In the Yoruba tradition, daily libations and offerings are made to honor ancestors and spirits, maintaining harmony between the living and the dead. These practices are not confined to specific religious days but are a continual part of life.

- **Cross-Cultural Connection**: Both Indian and African cultures view spirituality as a holistic way of life. The boundaries between the sacred and the everyday are fluid, with each culture emphasizing the need to live in harmony with the divine, ancestors, and nature. Daily rituals, whether through prayer, offerings, or communal gatherings, reflect a deep awareness of the spiritual forces at play in the world. This approach fosters a sense of interconnectedness, ensuring that spirituality is not abstract but an integral part of living, breathing existence.

The symbolic connections between Indian and African narratives are profound, with both cultures emphasizing the sacredness of nature, the transformative power of myth and archetypes, and the integration of spirituality into daily life. In both traditions, symbols such as rivers, trees, and archetypal figures like the hero and the trickster serve as bridges between the material and spiritual worlds, reminding us of the interconnectedness of all life. By examining these shared symbols, we see a reflection of universal human concerns—our place in the cosmos, the search for meaning, and the constant interplay between the seen and unseen.

4. Symbolism and Spirituality in Postcolonial Narratives

Postcolonial literature from both African and Indian contexts employs symbolism and spirituality as tools for cultural reclamation and resistance against colonial legacies. These narratives utilize traditional symbols not only to assert identity but also to navigate the complexities of modernity and the lingering effects of colonialism.

4.1 Reclaiming Cultural Identity

In the aftermath of colonialism, many writers have turned to their cultural heritage as a source of strength and identity. Symbolism plays a crucial role in this reclamation process, as it allows authors to express their cultural values, beliefs, and histories in a manner that resonates with contemporary audiences.

- **Chimamanda Ngozi Adichie**: In her novel *Half of a Yellow Sun*, Adichie uses symbols that connect her characters to their Igbo heritage, particularly during the Nigerian Civil War. The character Olanna's family home is a symbol of pre-colonial wealth and cultural identity. As Olanna navigates her life in a war-torn Nigeria, the house becomes a refuge that embodies her family's history and the resilience of her people. Adichie writes: "The house was filled with history, the kind that could be traced through the intricate carvings on the wooden doors and the way the sun fell in patterns on the polished floors." Here, the house symbolizes the continuity of cultural identity amidst chaos, representing a connection to the past and the enduring strength of heritage.
- **Buchi Emecheta**: In *The Joys of Womanhood*, Emecheta employs the symbol of the traditional Yoruba woman as a means of reclaiming identity. The protagonist, Nnu Ego, struggles between her traditional values and the pressures of colonial society. The significance of motherhood and the symbol of the "mother" in Yoruba culture serve as a foundation for Nnu Ego's identity. Emecheta writes: "A man cannot be without a woman, just as a woman cannot be without a man. But a woman

can be without a man if she has a child." This quote underscores the centrality of motherhood and the spiritual role of women in preserving cultural identity. Nnu Ego's journey reflects the struggle to assert her identity against the backdrop of colonialism, revealing the power of symbols tied to cultural heritage.

- **Raja Rao**: In *Kanthapura*, Raja Rao weaves the symbol of the *mothi* (pearl) into the narrative to represent purity and cultural richness. The protagonist, Moorthy, becomes a symbol of the spiritual awakening of the village, linking the community's identity to their cultural practices. Rao writes: "The pearl was not just a jewel; it was a reminder of our traditions, our purity, and our strength." Here, the pearl symbolizes the essence of Indian culture, highlighting the importance of reclaiming cultural identity in a rapidly changing world.

4.2 Spiritual Resistance

Spirituality in postcolonial narratives often manifests as a form of resistance against the dehumanizing effects of colonialism. Authors utilize spiritual symbols to reclaim agency and assert cultural pride, challenging colonial narratives that sought to undermine their identities.

- **Ngũgĩ wa Thiong'o**: In *Devil on the Cross*, Ngũgĩ employs the symbol of the *Gikuyu* (a sacred tree) as a representation of Kenyan culture and spirituality. The protagonist, Wariinga, experiences a spiritual awakening under the tree, which serves as a site of resistance against colonial oppression. Ngũgĩ writes: "The tree was a witness to our history, our pain, and our joy. It stood tall against the winds of colonialism, a reminder of who we are." The tree symbolizes the resilience of Kenyan culture and the spiritual strength of its people, serving as a metaphor for resistance against colonial forces that sought to erase their identity.

- **Wole Soyinka**: In *Death and the King's Horseman*, Soyinka uses the symbol of the *masquerade* to represent the spiritual connection between the living and the dead. The play explores the clash between colonial and traditional values, as the protagonist, Elesin, grapples with his duty to join his deceased king in the afterlife. Soyinka writes:"To deny the masquerade is to deny the truth of our existence. We are all bound by the cycles of life and death."This statement highlights the importance of spiritual rituals and symbols in maintaining cultural identity and resisting colonial narratives that undermine traditional practices.

- **Arundhati Roy**: In *The God of Small Things*, Roy uses the symbol of the river to convey spiritual resistance against social injustices. The river serves as a boundary between different worlds—rich and poor, accepted and rejected. The protagonist, Ammu, finds solace in the river, which symbolizes freedom and rebellion against societal norms. Roy writes: "The river held our secrets, our pain, and our desire for freedom. It was a sanctuary in a world that sought to confine us." The river embodies spiritual resilience, reflecting the characters' struggles against oppressive societal structures. It symbolizes the quest for liberation and the reclamation of identity in the face of colonial and social constraints.

In postcolonial narratives, symbolism and spirituality are powerful tools for reclaiming cultural identity and resisting colonial legacies. Through the exploration of symbols connected to heritage, tradition, and spirituality, writers like Adichie, Emecheta, Ngũgĩ, Soyinka, and Roy illuminate the profound ways in which cultural narratives can foster resilience and empowerment. These literary works serve as testaments to the enduring strength of identity, emphasizing that spirituality, deeply rooted in cultural symbols, can inspire hope and resistance in a postcolonial world.

The exploration of Indian and African narratives reveals a rich tapestry of spiritual connections, underpinned by shared symbols, archetypes, and an understanding of the sacredness of nature and everyday life. As diverse as these two cultures are, they converge on fundamental spiritual principles that speak to the universal human experience. This conclusion highlights the spiritual bridge between Indian and African cultures, emphasizing their shared values and perspectives.

1. Interconnectedness of Existence

At the heart of both Indian and African spiritual systems lies the profound understanding of interconnectedness. Life, death, nature, and the cosmos are seen as an intricate web of relationships where every being has a role to play. This interconnectedness fosters a sense of responsibility toward oneself, others, and the environment. Both cultures advocate for living in harmony with nature, recognizing that the health of the earth directly impacts human existence.

- **Example**: In Indian philosophy, the concept of *Ahimsa* (non-violence) extends beyond human interactions to encompass all living beings, promoting a deep respect for nature. Similarly, many African traditions view the land as sacred and deserving of care and protection, reflecting a symbiotic relationship with the environment.

2. The Role of Ancestors and Spiritual Guides

Ancestors hold a pivotal place in both Indian and African cultures, serving as spiritual guides and protectors. They are revered and honored through rituals, offerings, and storytelling, creating a continuous link between the living and the spiritual realm. This ancestral connection reinforces cultural identity and community cohesion, as individuals draw strength and wisdom from their forebears.

- **Example**: In Indian culture, rituals such as *Shraddha* are performed to honor ancestors and seek their blessings. Similarly, in many African societies, daily offerings and prayers to ancestors ensure their presence in the lives of the living, maintaining a dialogue that transcends time.

3. Spirituality in Everyday Life

Both cultures emphasize that spirituality is not limited to formal religious practices but is woven into the fabric of daily life. Rituals, community interactions, and acts of kindness are imbued with spiritual significance, highlighting the idea that every action carries moral and spiritual weight. This approach fosters a sense of mindfulness and intentionality, encouraging individuals to live with purpose and awareness.

- **Example**: The practice of communal gatherings in African societies, such as storytelling, dancing, and rituals, reflects a collective spirituality that strengthens bonds and fosters a shared sense of identity. In India, daily rituals like lighting lamps or offering food to deities serve as reminders of the divine presence in everyday activities.

4. Myth and Archetype as Universal Narratives

The myths and archetypes found in both Indian and African narratives serve as a vehicle for conveying universal truths about the human experience. These stories explore themes of heroism, sacrifice, love, and the quest for knowledge, resonating across cultural boundaries. They provide frameworks for understanding life's complexities and encourage individuals to navigate their journeys with resilience and wisdom.

- **Example**: The archetypal hero's journey in both cultures, whether represented by figures like Rama in Indian epics or Anansi in African folklore, reflects the challenges and triumphs of the human spirit, offering guidance and inspiration to navigate life's trials.

5. Cultural Exchange and Mutual Enrichment

The spiritual bridges between Indian and African cultures are not just limited to shared symbols and narratives; they also represent opportunities for cultural exchange and mutual enrichment. As globalization fosters interactions between diverse cultures, the sharing of spiritual practices, philosophies, and artistic expressions can lead to a deeper understanding of one another.

- **Example:** The influence of African rhythms and themes in Indian music and dance, as well as the incorporation of Indian philosophies in African spiritual practices, exemplifies how cultural exchange enriches both traditions, promoting appreciation and respect for diversity.

6. A Call for Global Unity

In an increasingly interconnected world, recognizing and celebrating the spiritual bridges between cultures can foster global unity and understanding. The shared values of interconnectedness, respect for nature, and the significance of spirituality in everyday life provide a foundation for addressing contemporary challenges, such as environmental degradation, social injustice, and cultural conflict.

- **Example:** Initiatives that promote intercultural dialogue, education, and collaboration can harness these spiritual connections to inspire collective action toward a more just and sustainable world.

The spiritual bridge between Indian and African cultures reflects a profound understanding of the interconnectedness of existence, the significance of ancestors, and the integration of spirituality into everyday life. Through shared symbols, archetypes, and narratives, these cultures offer rich insights into the human experience, celebrating the divine presence in nature and the importance of living with purpose and awareness. As we navigate the complexities of a diverse world, embracing these spiritual connections can foster mutual respect, cultural exchange, and a collective commitment to harmony, unity, and understanding. Ultimately, the exploration of these spiritual bridges serves as a reminder that, despite our differences, we are united by our shared humanity and the quest for meaning in our lives.

CHAPTER SIX

POST-COLONIAL NARRATIVES

Post-colonialism is a critical framework that emerged in the mid-20th century, focusing on the lasting impacts of colonialism on formerly colonized societies. It explores how colonial domination affected not only the political landscape but also the cultural, social, and personal identities of individuals within these societies. Post-colonialism scrutinizes how colonial power structures attempted to assert dominance over indigenous populations by reshaping cultural values, language, and history to reflect the ideologies of the colonizers. In essence, post-colonial studies serve as a lens through which we can examine the persistence of colonial structures and how these have been resisted, adapted, and, in some cases, reclaimed by post-colonial societies.

Historical Context: The origins of post-colonialism are closely tied to the decolonization movements of the mid-20th century, when numerous African, Asian, Caribbean, and Latin American countries gained independence from European powers. These movements triggered a wave of intellectual thought and literary expression that sought to deconstruct colonial ideologies and reassert indigenous identities. This period saw the emergence of influential thinkers, such as Frantz Fanon, Edward Said, and Gayatri Chakravorty Spivak, whose works provided new theoretical frameworks to analyze the cultural, political, and psychological impact of colonialism. Fanon's *The Wretched of the Earth* (1961) examined the psychological effects of colonization on individuals and communities, while Said's *Orientalism* (1978) exposed the Western portrayal of the "Orient" as a construct of colonial superiority and exoticism. Together, these thinkers influenced the discourse on post-colonialism, encouraging critical reflection on historical narratives and the power dynamics embedded within them.

Post-Colonial Literature as a Voice for the Marginalized: Post-colonial literature serves as a potent form of resistance and reclamation, providing a platform for voices that were silenced or distorted by colonial narratives. Writers from post-colonial backgrounds often use literature as a way to challenge stereotypes, reshape historical memories, and validate the experiences of marginalized communities. For example, Nigerian author Chinua Achebe's *Things Fall Apart* (1958) offers a counter-narrative to Western depictions of African societies, depicting the Igbo culture's rich traditions and the disruptions caused by colonial intrusion. Similarly, Caribbean writer Jean Rhys's *Wide Sargasso Sea* (1966) reinterprets Charlotte Brontë's *Jane Eyre* from the perspective of Bertha Mason, a character marginalized and demonized in the original work. These literary works illuminate the complex identities and layered experiences of post-colonial societies, questioning Western constructs and reimagining a history and identity that colonialism sought to suppress.

The Significance of Post-Colonial Narratives Today: In an era where globalization continues to impact cultural and individual identities, post-colonial narratives remain crucial. They foster an understanding of how colonial legacies still influence contemporary issues, such as race, migration, and identity politics. These narratives encourage readers to engage with diverse perspectives and critically examine how historical injustices manifest in the present. By highlighting the nuances of cultural exchange, resistance, and hybridity, post-colonial literature plays a vital role in broadening our understanding of the world and promoting a more inclusive global narrative.

In summary, post-colonial narratives stand as a powerful form of expression and critique, offering a space for previously marginalized voices to reassert their histories, identities, and cultural values. This chapter will explore the core themes, narrative techniques, and stylistic choices that define post-colonial literature, examining how these works resist colonial constructs and redefine cultural identities through storytelling. Through an exploration of identity, power, language, and hybridity, we can gain insight into the richness of post-colonial literature and its ongoing impact on both individual and collective understandings of self and society.

1. Core Themes in Post-Colonial Narratives
1.1 Identity and Hybridity

- **Overview**: The theme of identity is central to post-colonial literature, where characters often grapple with questions of selfhood in the aftermath of colonization. Colonial rule disrupted indigenous cultures, imposing foreign values, languages, and belief systems that fragmented personal and collective identities. As individuals and societies navigate the space between colonial influence and indigenous roots, they often find themselves embodying *hybridity*, a concept defined by post-colonial theorist Homi Bhabha as the blending of two cultures to create something unique.

- **The Third Space**: Bhabha's "Third Space" suggests that post-colonial identity is neither fully indigenous nor entirely colonial, but exists in a liminal state that merges elements of both. This hybridity allows individuals to forge a new sense of self that incorporates, yet challenges, colonial constructs. For example, in *The Mimic Men* by V.S. Naipaul, the protagonist struggles with identity in a colonial society, trying to reconcile his mixed heritage and the values imposed by British rule. Hybridity offers both opportunities and conflicts as characters seek authenticity in a world where their cultural background has been altered by colonial dominance.

1.2 Resistance and Empowerment

- **Reclaiming Voice and Narrative**: Post-colonial literature is often a space for reclaiming voice and agency that were suppressed during colonial rule. Many post-colonial narratives empower characters to resist oppression through acts of cultural preservation, political activism, or personal rebellion. Resistance in these narratives can range from overt defiance, such as in the works of Ngũgĩ wa Thiong'o, who wrote in his native Kikuyu to oppose linguistic colonialism, to subtle subversions, like choosing local cultural practices over imposed foreign ones.

- **Decolonizing the Mind**: Ngũgĩ wa Thiong'o's concept of "decolonizing the mind" explores how literature can be a means of psychological and cultural liberation. By writing in native languages and celebrating indigenous customs, post-colonial authors resist the dominance of Western ideals and reclaim their own identities. This theme of empowerment through cultural reclamation is vividly seen in *Things Fall Apart* by Chinua Achebe, which portrays Igbo society's rich traditions and resilience in the face of colonial incursion, challenging the portrayal of African cultures as primitive or inferior.

1.3 Diaspora and Migration

- **Themes of Displacement and Alienation**: The colonial experience created global diasporas as people migrated in search of better opportunities or were forcibly displaced. Diasporic characters in post-colonial narratives often experience a sense of *double consciousness*, where they must navigate between their native culture and the dominant culture in their new environment. This theme highlights the emotional complexity of belonging and alienation, as seen in *The Namesake* by Jhumpa Lahiri, where the protagonist struggles with identity and cultural heritage while growing up in America.
- **Longing and Nostalgia**: Migration often brings a sense of loss and nostalgia for the homeland, as characters experience cultural and familial separation. Post-colonial literature frequently explores these feelings, portraying how displaced individuals maintain

connections to their roots while adapting to a new identity. Salman Rushdie's *Midnight's Children* delves into the nostalgic bond with one's homeland, where characters grapple with a fragmented identity as they balance their past and present selves.

1.4 Language and Power

- **Language as a Tool of Oppression and Resistance**: Language plays a complex role in post-colonial narratives, acting both as a symbol of colonial dominance and a vehicle for resistance. Colonizers often imposed their language on native populations, which served to undermine indigenous cultures and reinforce control. In *A Tempest*, Aimé Césaire reimagines Shakespeare's *The Tempest*, transforming Caliban into a symbol of linguistic and cultural resistance who demands the right to express himself in his language.
- **Writing Back in the Colonial Language**: Many post-colonial authors use the language of the colonizer to subvert it from within, effectively "writing back" to the empire. By reappropriating the colonizer's language, these authors redefine it to express indigenous experiences and realities. This is evident in Jean Rhys's *Wide Sargasso Sea*, which reinterprets the story of Bertha Mason, the "madwoman in the attic" from *Jane Eyre*, giving her voice and humanity in a language previously used to marginalize her.

1.5 Trauma and Memory

- **Collective and Personal Memory**: Colonization inflicted deep trauma on societies, communities, and individuals, often erasing cultural memories and replacing them with distorted histories. Post-colonial literature frequently addresses this theme, portraying characters who struggle with the psychological scars of colonial violence. *Beloved* by Toni Morrison, though rooted in the American post-slavery context, resonates within post-colonial studies for its exploration of inherited trauma and the haunting presence of the past.

- **Reclaiming History and Memory**: Memory is a means of resistance, allowing post-colonial characters to recover and retell their histories. Many authors focus on collective memory as a way to honor cultural legacies and counter the erasure wrought by colonial rule. In *One Hundred Years of Solitude* by Gabriel Garcia Marquez, magical realism is employed to represent the memories and myths of Latin America, preserving cultural narratives that colonialism sought to overwrite.

1.6 Cultural Reclamation and Authenticity

- **Reviving Suppressed Traditions**: Post-colonial narratives often strive to recover traditions, stories, and practices that were suppressed or erased by colonialism. Through folklore, myth, and religion, authors resurrect indigenous knowledge systems, reaffirming the value of native cultural expressions. For instance, Ben Okri's *The Famished Road* draws heavily from Yoruba mythology, blending it into a narrative that resists Western rationalism and celebrates African spirituality.
- **Questioning Authenticity and Essentialism**: While some characters pursue cultural authenticity, post-colonial narratives also critique essentialist notions of culture, where identities are seen as fixed or "pure."

This theme is particularly evident in Kiran Desai's *The Inheritance of Loss*, where characters navigate a multicultural, globalized world that blurs traditional cultural boundaries. The narrative reveals the complexity of cultural identity, showing that authenticity is often an evolving, multifaceted concept.

1.7 Gender and Patriarchy

- **Intersection of Gender and Colonialism**: Colonialism not only disrupted societies but also imposed patriarchal structures that marginalized women in both indigenous and colonial societies. Post-colonial literature frequently explores how colonial rule intensified gender inequalities, leading female characters to confront both colonial oppression and patriarchal control. Buchi Emecheta's *The Joys of Motherhood* examines the pressures on African women to conform to traditional gender roles while navigating the effects of colonial modernity.
- **Female Empowerment and Resistance**: Female characters in post-colonial literature often embody resilience and agency, challenging both colonial and patriarchal oppression. These narratives celebrate women's strength and the complexity of their struggles, as in Tsitsi Dangarembga's *Nervous Conditions*, where the protagonist defies gender expectations in pursuit of education and self-discovery.

The core themes in post-colonial narratives are woven into a rich tapestry that captures the complexity of identity, power, and culture in societies marked by colonial influence. From the struggle for authenticity to the reclamation of history and the navigation of hybrid identities, post-colonial literature provides a nuanced exploration of human experience in the post-colonial world. Through these themes, post-colonial narratives continue to challenge readers, inviting them to engage with diverse perspectives and the realities of formerly colonized societies in their quest for cultural and personal liberation.

2. Narrative Techniques and Stylistic Features

2.1 Magic Realism

- **Blending the Ordinary and the Extraordinary**: Magic realism is a narrative technique that merges realistic settings with magical or supernatural elements. This style enables post-colonial authors to depict the indigenous worldview, where the spiritual and physical realms coexist. Unlike Western rationalist frameworks, magic realism reflects a cultural belief system in which myths, legends, and spiritual phenomena are integral to reality. Gabriel Garcia Marquez's *One Hundred Years of Solitude* is a seminal work in this genre, where magical occurrences are woven into the everyday lives of characters, symbolizing the region's complex history and cultural narratives.

- **Subversion of Colonial Realism**: By blending fantasy with realism, post-colonial writers subvert the colonial insistence on empirical truth and objective reality. Authors like Ben Okri, in *The Famished Road*, use magic realism to capture African spirituality and the coexistence of multiple realities. This style rejects Western conventions of truth, instead prioritizing indigenous perspectives that emphasize mystery and the interconnectedness of all things.

2.2 Oral Tradition and Storytelling

- **Incorporation of Folklore, Myth, and Proverbs**: Many post-colonial works draw heavily from oral traditions, integrating folklore, myth, and proverbs to preserve cultural heritage and affirm indigenous storytelling methods. This narrative technique allows authors to honor traditional knowledge systems and resist the erasure of oral cultures by written colonial records. Chinua Achebe's *Things Fall Apart* makes extensive use of proverbs, which reflect the wisdom of the Igbo culture and give the narrative a uniquely African cadence.

- **Communal and Non-Linear Storytelling**: Oral storytelling often follows a non-linear, episodic structure that emphasizes communal memory over individual experience. Post-colonial narratives such as Ngũgĩ wa Thiong'o's *Petals of Blood* employ a cyclical structure, which mirrors oral traditions that revisit the past to interpret the present. This technique disrupts Western narrative linearity, instead portraying history as a shared, evolving experience.

2.3 Polyphony and Multiple Perspectives

- **Voices of the Marginalized**: Post-colonial narratives frequently employ polyphony, or the inclusion of multiple voices and perspectives, to reflect the diversity and complexity of post-colonial societies. This technique challenges the monolithic narrative imposed by colonial powers and provides a platform for various marginalized voices. In Salman Rushdie's *Midnight's*

Children, multiple narrators and conflicting perspectives create a cacophony of voices that convey the chaotic and pluralistic nature of post-colonial India.

- **Challenging Authority**: By presenting competing viewpoints, post-colonial writers invite readers to question authoritative voices and official histories. This narrative style resists singular truths, instead embracing the multiplicity of experience. Tsitsi Dangarembga's *Nervous Conditions* features the perspectives of several women whose narratives highlight diverse challenges within Zimbabwean society, demonstrating how post-colonial identity is multifaceted and often fragmented.

2.4 Use of Creole, Pidgin, and Vernacular Languages

- **Subversion of Colonial Language**: Language is a powerful tool in post-colonial literature, where the use of Creole, pidgin, or local vernacular challenges the hegemony of colonial languages and asserts the value of indigenous dialects. This stylistic choice allows characters to speak authentically and disrupts the reader's expectation of "proper" English. Jean Rhys's *Wide Sargasso Sea* utilizes Caribbean Creole to lend authenticity to its setting and to contrast the voices of the colonizer and the colonized.
- **Reclaiming Linguistic Identity**: By writing in their own languages or adapting the colonizer's language to suit their needs, post-colonial writers reclaim linguistic identity and resist cultural erasure. Ngũgĩ wa Thiong'o's decision to write in Kikuyu reflects this commitment to linguistic reclamation. The use of native languages can also symbolize solidarity with local readers and the

preservation of cultural memory.

2.5 Intertextuality and Rewriting of Colonial Texts

- **"Writing Back" to the Canon**: Many post-colonial authors engage with canonical Western texts, reinterpreting and reimagining them from a post-colonial perspective. This technique, often referred to as "writing back," challenges the assumptions and representations within colonial literature. For instance, Jean Rhys's *Wide Sargasso Sea* serves as a prequel to Charlotte Brontë's *Jane Eyre*, reclaiming the narrative of Bertha Mason, who was marginalized and dehumanized in the original text.
- **Subverting Colonial Narratives**: By rewriting colonial texts, post-colonial authors expose biases and critique the imperialist ideologies embedded in Western literature. *Foe* by J.M. Coetzee reimagines Daniel Defoe's *Robinson Crusoe* from the perspective of a female narrator, questioning colonial myths of exploration and conquest. Intertextuality thus allows post-colonial writers to confront the "master narratives" of colonialism and offer alternative histories.

2.6 Fragmented and Non-Linear Narratives

- **Reflecting Psychological Dislocation**: Many post-colonial narratives adopt fragmented or non-linear structures to convey the disorienting effects of colonization on individuals and societies. Characters often experience temporal dislocation, where past and present merge to reveal trauma, memory, and loss. This structure mirrors the fractured identities and cultural dissonance that colonization often produces. In *Beloved* by Toni Morrison, the non-linear narrative structure reflects the traumatic legacy of slavery and how it haunts both personal and collective memory.

- **Challenging Western Chronology**: Non-linear narratives also resist Western notions of time and history, which often prioritize progress and linearity. Instead, these works emphasize cyclical time, where events repeat or are revisited, aligning with indigenous understandings of history as circular rather than sequential. Ben Okri's *The Famished Road* uses a cyclical structure, portraying the timeless journey of Azaro, a spirit child who moves between worlds in a way that reflects traditional African cosmology.

2.7 Symbolism and Allegory

- **Symbols of Resistance and Survival**: Post-colonial literature often employs symbols to represent complex themes of resistance, resilience, and survival. These symbols carry cultural and political weight, highlighting how characters navigate power dynamics. In Chinua Achebe's *Things Fall Apart*, the breaking of the kola nut symbolizes community, tradition, and the social cohesion of the Igbo society, all of which are threatened by colonial intrusion.
- **Allegorical Representations of Colonial Experience**: Post-colonial narratives frequently employ allegory to encapsulate the larger colonial experience. In *The Shadow Lines* by Amitav Ghosh, the narrator's fragmented memories and the blurred borders between nations symbolize the fluidity and artificiality of colonial boundaries. Allegory enables authors to layer

multiple meanings within their works, inviting readers to interpret historical, cultural, and social messages beyond the immediate narrative.

2.8 The Use of Silence and the Unspoken

- **Silence as Resistance**: Silence and omission can function as forms of resistance in post-colonial narratives, where unsaid words and suppressed thoughts reveal the limitations imposed by colonial rule. By withholding certain details or allowing characters to remain silent, authors emphasize the gaps and erasures caused by colonial violence. In *A Passage to India* by E.M. Forster, the silence of certain characters reflects the unbridgeable divide between colonizers and the colonized.
- **The Unspoken Trauma**: Silence also conveys the weight of trauma and the unspeakable experiences left by colonization. Toni Morrison's *Beloved* often dwells on what characters cannot bring themselves to say, highlighting the emotional burden of slavery's legacy. In post-colonial literature, silence and absence serve as powerful narrative tools, signifying the suppressed voices and memories that lie beneath the surface of colonial history.

The narrative techniques and stylistic features in post-colonial literature are crafted to challenge colonial constructs, celebrate cultural heritage, and communicate the complex legacies of colonialism. From magic realism to intertextuality, these techniques enable post-colonial authors to create immersive worlds that reflect the nuances of post-colonial identities. Through storytelling rooted in indigenous knowledge, reimagined canonical texts, and fragmented structures, post-colonial literature reshapes our understanding of history, culture, and identity, offering readers a richer, more inclusive narrative landscape.

3. Case Studies of Key Texts

3.1 *Things Fall Apart* by Chinua Achebe

- **Overview**: Widely considered a cornerstone of African post-colonial literature, Achebe's *Things Fall Apart* examines the collision between traditional Igbo culture and British colonial forces. Set in pre-colonial Nigeria, it tells the story of Okonkwo, a respected village leader whose world begins to unravel with the arrival of European missionaries.
- **Themes of Cultural Conflict and Identity**: The novel vividly portrays the tensions between tradition and change. Okonkwo embodies traditional Igbo values, which are threatened by the encroachment of colonial influence. Achebe presents a nuanced perspective on pre-colonial life, highlighting its complexity and value, countering colonial depictions of African societies as primitive.
- **Narrative Techniques**:

  - **Integration of Igbo Proverbs and Folktales**: Achebe incorporates Igbo proverbs and folklore, grounding the narrative in the local culture and resisting colonial language norms. Proverbs, like "A man who makes trouble for others is also making trouble for himself," add cultural depth and affirm indigenous knowledge systems.
  - **Use of Tragic Structure**: Okonkwo's tragic fall echoes classic literary tragedies, which Achebe

adapts to a uniquely African context, challenging Western literary forms. This tragic arc conveys the devastation that colonialism brings to indigenous communities, using Okonkwo's personal loss as a microcosm of collective cultural destruction.

3.2 *Wide Sargasso Sea* by Jean Rhys

- **Overview**: *Wide Sargasso Sea* reinterprets the story of Bertha Mason, the "madwoman in the attic" from Charlotte Brontë's *Jane Eyre*, giving her a voice and exploring her background as Antoinette Cosway, a Creole woman in Jamaica. Rhys's novel examines the intersection of race, gender, and colonialism, questioning colonial narratives about Caribbean people.
- **Themes of Identity, Madness, and Colonial Oppression**: Rhys presents Antoinette's descent into madness as a result of cultural alienation, racial prejudice, and gender oppression. The novel explores how colonial stereotypes dehumanize individuals and destabilize identities, especially when they don't conform to binary racial categorizations.
- **Narrative Techniques**:

  - **Dual Perspectives**: The narrative shifts between Antoinette and her English husband, revealing the clash of perspectives and misinterpretations that define their relationship. This technique emphasizes how colonial power dynamics distort individual understanding and relationships.
  - **Use of Creole and Local Dialects**: Rhys uses Creole speech and local Jamaican references to anchor the novel in Caribbean culture, resisting British linguistic

norms and challenging the Eurocentric lens of *Jane Eyre.*

3.3 *Midnight's Children* by Salman Rushdie

- **Overview**: This epic novel chronicles the lives of children born on the stroke of midnight on August 15, 1947, the day of India's independence from Britain. Narrated by Saleem Sinai, who possesses telepathic powers, *Midnight's Children* blends magical realism with historical events to explore post-colonial identity in India.
- **Themes of National Identity and Hybridity**: The novel represents the fractured identity of post-colonial India, where multiple religions, languages, and cultures coexist but also clash. Saleem's telepathic connection with other "midnight's children" symbolizes the diversity and division within the new nation.
- **Narrative Techniques**:

  ○ **Magic Realism**: Rushdie uses magic realism to intertwine historical events with the supernatural, portraying India's cultural richness and complexity. This technique resists Western realism, embracing Indian myth and folklore as legitimate expressions of truth.
  ○ **Non-Linear Structure and Fragmentation**: The novel's fragmented structure reflects the chaotic, often contradictory nature of post-colonial identity. Saleem's non-linear narration, where he revisits events and connects disparate moments, mirrors the disjointed national identity that emerges post-independence.

3.4 *The God of Small Things* by Arundhati Roy

- **Overview:** Set in Kerala, India, *The God of Small Things* tells the story of the Ipe family, whose lives are shaped by love, social norms, and traumatic events. Through the lives of fraternal twins Rahel and Estha, Roy examines how caste, colonial legacies, and family structures affect individual agency.
- **Themes of Social Oppression and Forbidden Love:** The novel critiques caste discrimination, social hierarchy, and the lingering impact of colonialism on Indian society. Forbidden relationships, such as the love between Ammu and Velutha, a Dalit man, expose the brutal enforcement of caste and class norms.
- **Narrative Techniques:**

  - **Non-Linear Chronology:** Roy's story moves between different timelines, unraveling the family's trauma piece by piece. This disjointed timeline reflects the fragmented memories of the twins and highlights the lasting impact of traumatic events.
  - **Symbolism and Lyrical Prose:** Roy's rich, poetic language and use of symbolism (such as the river that runs through the family estate) add layers to the narrative. Her style evokes the beauty of Kerala's natural landscape while symbolizing the complexity of the social issues the novel addresses.

3.5 *Beloved* by Toni Morrison

- **Overview:** Though set in the American post-slavery context, Morrison's *Beloved* is often analyzed within post-colonial frameworks for its exploration of trauma, memory, and the legacy of enslavement. The novel tells the story of Sethe, an escaped slave haunted by the spirit of her deceased daughter.

- **Themes of Trauma and Memory**: Morrison delves into the deep, haunting effects of slavery, portraying how characters are haunted by memories that disrupt their attempts to move forward. *Beloved* illustrates how the violence of colonization affects generations, echoing the experiences of other post-colonial societies.

- **Narrative Techniques**:

  - **Stream of Consciousness**: Morrison's use of stream-of-consciousness narration allows readers to experience the raw, often fragmented memories of the characters, reflecting the enduring trauma of slavery.

  - **Use of Silence and the Unspoken**: Much of the trauma in *Beloved* is expressed through what is left unsaid, with silence symbolizing the weight of unspeakable memories. Morrison employs gaps and omissions, leaving readers to piece together painful histories, reflecting the complexities of intergenerational trauma.

3.6 *The Inheritance of Loss* by Kiran Desai

- **Overview**: Set in the northeastern Himalayas, *The Inheritance of Loss* intertwines the lives of characters in India and America, addressing issues of migration, globalization, and cultural alienation. The narrative juxtaposes the experiences of Sai, an orphaned girl in India, and Biju, an undocumented Indian immigrant in New York City.

- **Themes of Globalization and Cultural Displacement**: Desai examines the consequences of globalization, where characters navigate cultural displacement and long for a sense of belonging. The novel highlights the post-colonial struggles of identity and self-worth amid changing economic landscapes.
- **Narrative Techniques**:

  - **Multiple Perspectives**: By presenting various perspectives across continents, Desai underscores the shared yet distinct experiences of individuals affected by colonial legacies and modern globalization. The parallel stories of Sai and Biju illustrate the complex impact of migration and cultural fragmentation.
  - **Irony and Subtle Satire**: Desai employs irony to critique the romanticization of Western culture and the pursuit of "better" lives in foreign countries. This technique exposes the harsh realities of cultural alienation and the ironic futility of Western ideals.

3.7 *Season of Migration to the North* by Tayeb Salih

- **Overview**: This Sudanese novel follows the narrator, a young man returning to his village after studying in Europe, and his encounter with Mustafa Sa'eed, a mysterious figure who has lived in England. The novel examines the psychological impact of colonization and the complex relationships between East and West.
- **Themes of Cultural Clash and the Exoticized Other**: Through Mustafa's character, Salih explores the colonial fetishization of the "Orient" and the lasting scars of cultural alienation. Mustafa's experiences in Europe

reflect the power dynamics of colonial relationships, where he oscillates between attraction to and rejection of Western culture.

- **Narrative Techniques:**

  - **Dual Narrative**: The story alternates between the perspectives of the narrator and Mustafa, creating a dialogue between two generations shaped by colonial influence. This duality highlights the ongoing impact of colonialism on personal and cultural identity.
  - **Psychological Realism and Allegory**: Salih blends psychological depth with allegorical elements, using Mustafa's character as a symbol of post-colonial alienation and the psychological costs of colonial encounters. The narrative's layered meanings invite readers to explore identity, power, and resistance on multiple levels.

4. Theoretical Approaches in Post-Colonial Criticism
4.1 Edward Said's Orientalism

- **Core Concept**: Edward Said's concept of "Orientalism" addresses the Western perception and portrayal of the East as an exotic, backward, and uncivilized "Other." In his seminal work, *Orientalism* (1978), Said argues that this portrayal was not only a cultural bias but a method of control, allowing the West to justify and maintain its dominance over Eastern societies.
- **Application in Literature**: Said's framework has been used to analyze how colonial and post-colonial texts depict non-Western societies. In Western literary works, the "Orient" is often depicted as inferior or mysterious. For example, *A Passage to India* by E.M.

Forster presents a British perspective on India that reflects both fascination with and condescension toward Indian culture.

- **Significance**: Orientalism critiques the underlying power structures in Western depictions of the East, revealing how literary representation can reinforce colonial ideologies. Post-colonial writers use this critique to deconstruct colonial stereotypes and challenge Western hegemonic narratives.

4.2 Homi K. Bhabha's Concept of Hybridity

- **Core Concept**: Homi K. Bhabha's concept of hybridity explores the "in-between" spaces created by colonial encounters, where cultures merge and new, hybrid identities are formed. In his work *The Location of Culture* (1994), Bhabha argues that hybridity destabilizes fixed notions of identity, power, and culture, creating an "ambivalent" space that both disrupts and reinvents colonial dominance.
- **Application in Literature**: Hybridity is frequently employed to analyze post-colonial characters who straddle multiple cultures. For instance, in Salman Rushdie's *The Satanic Verses*, characters like Gibreel Farishta and Saladin Chamcha embody hybrid identities, navigating their connections to both Britain and India. This hybridity disrupts the binary opposition of colonizer and colonized, emphasizing the fluidity of post-colonial identity.
- **Significance**: Hybridity challenges the purity of cultural identities imposed by colonialism, highlighting the cultural syncretism that emerges from colonial encounters. Bhabha's theory has been instrumental in

analyzing the complexities of identity and the spaces where power and resistance intersect.

4.3 Gayatri Chakravorty Spivak's Subaltern Studies

- **Core Concept**: Gayatri Spivak, a key figure in post-colonial theory, introduced the concept of the "subaltern" to refer to marginalized groups who lack a voice in dominant historical narratives. In her influential essay "Can the Subaltern Speak?" (1988), Spivak argues that the voices of the oppressed are often either silenced or co-opted by the dominant discourse, making it challenging to represent their experiences authentically.
- **Application in Literature**: Spivak's theory is applied to analyze marginalized characters who are denied agency within colonial and post-colonial narratives. In Chinua Achebe's *Things Fall Apart*, for example, the voices of women and lower-caste individuals remain largely unheard, illustrating the limitations of traditional power structures. Similarly, in *The God of Small Things* by Arundhati Roy, the Dalit character Velutha's experience reflects subaltern silencing, as societal structures prevent him from having a voice.
- **Significance**: Subaltern studies emphasize the need for ethical representation of the oppressed in post-colonial literature. Spivak's work challenges critics to consider whose voices are included and whose are excluded, prompting questions about agency, identity, and historical memory.

4.4 Frantz Fanon's Psychology of Colonization

- **Core Concept**: Frantz Fanon's work on the psychological effects of colonization, particularly in *Black Skin, White Masks* (1952) and *The Wretched of the Earth* (1961), addresses how colonialism affects the mental health and identity of the colonized. Fanon explores how the colonized internalize the belief in their own inferiority and how colonial oppression disrupts their sense of self.

- **Application in Literature**: Fanon's ideas on internalized oppression are often used to examine post-colonial characters grappling with identity and inferiority complexes. In Jean Rhys's *Wide Sargasso Sea*, Antoinette's struggle with her Creole identity and her alienation from both European and Caribbean societies echoes Fanon's exploration of alienation. Similarly, in *Season of Migration to the North* by Tayeb Salih, the character Mustafa Sa'eed embodies Fanon's concept of psychological conflict as he confronts his identity in post-colonial Sudan.

- **Significance**: Fanon's work highlights the profound psychological impact of colonial rule, shedding light on issues such as self-worth, identity crisis, and the challenge of decolonization. His ideas encourage a deeper examination of character psychology and internal conflict in post-colonial narratives.

4.5 The Concept of Mimicry and Ambivalence by Homi K. Bhabha

- **Core Concept**: Mimicry, as introduced by Bhabha, refers to the colonized subject's imitation of the colonizer's culture, language, and customs. However, this mimicry is ambivalent; it is both a strategy of survival and a form of resistance that exposes the fragility of colonial authority. Through mimicry, the colonized disrupts the ideal image of the colonizer, as mimicry is never complete and often distorts the original.

- **Application in Literature**: In *The Mimic Men* by V.S. Naipaul, the protagonist, Ranjit Kripal Singh, adopts the behaviors and attitudes of the British colonizers, yet his imitation reveals a sense of displacement and identity crisis. This incomplete mimicry serves as a critique of colonial power structures. Similarly, in *Nervous Conditions* by Tsitsi Dangarembga, characters like Nyasha and Tambu grapple with mimicry, as they navigate Western education and cultural norms.
- **Significance**: Bhabha's concept of mimicry underscores the ambivalence and contradictions within colonial identity, revealing how imitation both reinforces and destabilizes colonial authority. It is a useful lens for examining how post-colonial characters assert agency through partial identification with the colonizer.

4.6 Post-Colonial Eco-Criticism

- **Core Concept**: Post-colonial eco-criticism examines how colonialism has affected the environment and how post-colonial texts reflect these ecological impacts. This approach explores how colonial exploitation of resources and land degradation continues to affect formerly colonized regions and peoples, linking environmental destruction with cultural and political oppression.
- **Application in Literature**: In *The Hungry Tide* by Amitav Ghosh, the Sundarbans landscape is both a site of beauty and struggle, depicting how colonial

exploitation has left a lasting environmental impact. Additionally, the indigenous communities' relationship with their environment contrasts with the Western view of nature as a resource to be controlled and exploited.

- **Significance**: This approach links environmental issues with colonial histories, highlighting how ecological degradation is intertwined with cultural erasure and economic exploitation. Post-colonial eco-criticism has gained relevance as environmental justice becomes a critical aspect of global discourse, drawing attention to indigenous knowledge and sustainable practices.

4.7 Dependency Theory and Neo-Colonialism

- **Core Concept**: Dependency theory examines the economic relationships between former colonies and colonial powers, suggesting that political independence does not necessarily translate into economic autonomy. Neo-colonialism describes the ways in which former colonial powers continue to exert control over these nations through economic means, perpetuating cycles of dependence and poverty.
- **Application in Literature**: Works like Ngũgĩ wa Thiong'o's *Petals of Blood* address the socio-economic exploitation in post-independence Kenya, where local resources are controlled by foreign interests, leaving communities impoverished. In *The Inheritance of Loss* by Kiran Desai, characters struggle with economic dependency and cultural alienation, reflecting how globalization and neo-colonialism perpetuate inequality.

- **Significance**: This approach highlights the economic dimensions of post-colonialism, showing how financial dependence can undermine political sovereignty. By focusing on economic injustice, post-colonial literature critiques the lingering inequalities that persist long after political independence is achieved.

4.8 Post-Colonial Feminism

- **Core Concept**: Post-colonial feminism addresses the unique intersection of gender, race, and colonial history, arguing that mainstream feminism often overlooks the specific struggles of women in post-colonial societies. This approach critiques Western feminist perspectives that may impose their own cultural norms on non-Western women, without recognizing the distinct challenges posed by colonial histories.
- **Application in Literature**: Post-colonial feminist readings focus on how female characters navigate patriarchal oppression exacerbated by colonial structures. In *Nervous Conditions* by Tsitsi Dangarembga, Tambu's journey reflects her struggle for education and autonomy in a society that is both patriarchal and shaped by colonial legacies. Buchi Emecheta's *The Joys of Motherhood* also explores how Nigerian women are affected by colonial economic policies that alter family structures and gender roles.
- **Significance**: Post-colonial feminism emphasizes the importance of cultural context in understanding gender oppression and advocates for a more inclusive approach to feminism. It highlights how colonial histories intersect with local traditions, challenging one-size-fits-all models of feminism that often fail to address the

complexities of women's lived experiences in diverse cultural settings. By foregrounding the unique challenges faced by women in post-colonial societies, this framework underscores the necessity of recognizing historical injustices and the ongoing effects of colonialism on gender dynamics. It critiques dominant feminist narratives that may inadvertently perpetuate neo-colonial attitudes, calling for a re-evaluation of what constitutes feminist solidarity. This perspective not only enriches feminist discourse but also fosters a deeper understanding of how global power structures shape individual lives. Moreover, post-colonial feminism seeks to amplify marginalized voices, advocating for a pluralistic approach that respects and incorporates local knowledge systems, thus enabling a more nuanced dialogue about women's rights and agency. In doing so, it promotes an intersectional analysis that considers the interplay of race, class, and gender, ultimately leading to more effective strategies for resistance and empowerment across different cultural landscapes.

4.8.1 Decolonizing Feminism

- **Overview**: Post-colonial feminism seeks to decolonize feminist discourse by challenging the Eurocentric narratives that dominate mainstream feminism. It emphasizes the need to understand women's experiences within the context of their specific cultural, historical, and social backgrounds. This involves recognizing that the struggles faced by women in post-colonial societies cannot be fully understood through a Western feminist lens, which often prioritizes issues of gender over race, class, and colonial histories.

- **Implications**: This theme underscores the importance of intersectionality, advocating for a feminism that incorporates the voices and experiences of women from diverse cultural backgrounds. Post-colonial feminists argue that true liberation for women can only be achieved when colonial histories and ongoing neocolonial practices are critically examined.

4.8.2 Resistance and Agency

- **Overview**: Post-colonial feminist discourse often highlights the active resistance of women against patriarchal and colonial structures. It emphasizes that women are not merely victims of oppression but are agents of change in their societies. This resistance can take many forms, including cultural production, political activism, and social movements.
- **Examples in Literature**: In her novel *The Joys of Motherhood*, Buchi Emecheta portrays the protagonist, Nnu Ego, as a complex character who struggles against both colonial and patriarchal systems. Nnu Ego's journey illustrates the ways in which women navigate their roles as mothers while asserting their identities and resisting oppression. Similarly, in *So Long a Letter* by Mariama Bâ, the protagonist Ramatoulaye reflects on her life and challenges societal expectations, illustrating the resilience and agency of women in the face of adversity.

Critiques of Post-Colonial Feminism
4.8.3 Essentialism and Representation

- **Overview**: One critique of post-colonial feminism is the potential for essentialism, where women from different cultural backgrounds are homogenized or stereotyped based on their gender. Critics argue that this can lead to oversimplified portrayals that fail to account for the diversity of women's experiences within a given cultural context.
- **Response**: Post-colonial feminists address this critique by emphasizing the importance of intersectionality and the need for nuanced representations of women. They advocate for inclusive narratives that reflect the complexities of women's identities, acknowledging that factors such as class, ethnicity, and sexuality intersect with gender in shaping individual experiences.

4.8.4 The Role of Western Feminism

- **Overview**: Post-colonial feminists often critique Western feminist movements for their tendency to impose their frameworks and solutions on non-Western women. This can result in a paternalistic approach that overlooks the specific struggles and cultural contexts of women in post-colonial societies.
- **Examples**: The debate surrounding the representation of Muslim women in Western media illustrates this critique. Many post-colonial feminists argue that Western portrayals often reinforce stereotypes, failing to capture the agency and diverse experiences of Muslim women. Writers like Lila Abu-Lughod challenge these narratives by calling for a more nuanced understanding of women's lives that recognizes their agency within their cultural contexts.

Contemporary Voices in Post-Colonial Feminism
4.8.5 Key Thinkers

- **Chandra Talpade Mohanty**: In her influential essay "Under Western Eyes: Feminist Scholarship and Colonial Discourses" (1984), Mohanty critiques the portrayal of Third World women as a monolithic group lacking agency. She calls for an understanding of women's struggles within specific historical and cultural contexts, advocating for solidarity among women that transcends borders while acknowledging their unique experiences.

- **Ania Loomba**: Loomba's work in *Colonialism/Postcolonialism* emphasizes the interconnectedness of colonialism and gender, arguing that understanding women's experiences requires analyzing both gender and colonial dynamics. She highlights how colonial histories have shaped gender relations, making it essential to consider these intersections in feminist discourse.

- **Amina Mama**: Mama's scholarship focuses on the intersection of gender, race, and class in African contexts. She critiques both colonial and post-colonial power structures, advocating for a feminist perspective that is rooted in the realities of African women's lives. Mama emphasizes the need for African women to define their struggles and priorities within feminist movements.

4.8.6 Contemporary Literature and Feminism

- **Chimamanda Ngozi Adichie**: In works like *Half of a Yellow Sun* and *Americanah*, Adichie addresses the complexities of gender and identity within the Nigerian context. Her narratives explore the impact of colonial legacies on women's lives and the ways in which they assert their agency in patriarchal societies.

- **Kiran Desai**: In *The Inheritance of Loss*, Desai weaves together themes of migration, identity, and gender, exploring the lives of women navigating the challenges of post-colonial realities. Her characters grapple with their identities in a globalized world, highlighting the intersection of gender and cultural displacement.

- **Arundhati Roy**: In her works, particularly *The God of Small Things*, Roy delves into the intersections of caste, gender, and colonial history. Her narratives reflect the experiences of women in post-colonial India, emphasizing their agency while critiquing oppressive societal structures.

Post-colonial feminism offers a vital framework for understanding the complexities of gender, race, and colonial histories in contemporary literature. By deconstructing Eurocentric narratives, advocating for intersectionality, and emphasizing women's agency, post-colonial feminists contribute to a richer understanding of the diverse experiences of women in post-colonial societies. As the field evolves, it continues to grapple with challenges related to representation, essentialism, and the need for ethical engagement, ensuring that the voices of women from all backgrounds are heard and valued in the ongoing discourse of feminism and post-colonial studies.

5. Contemporary Perspectives and Challenges

5.1 Globalization and Cultural Hybridization

- **Overview**: Globalization has transformed cultural exchanges, leading to increased interconnectedness across the globe. This has resulted in cultural hybridization, where elements from various cultures blend, creating new forms of expression and identity. Post-colonial literature now frequently addresses the implications of globalization, exploring how cultural identities evolve in response to global influences.

- **Contemporary Perspective**: Authors like Chimamanda Ngozi Adichie and Salman Rushdie examine how globalization affects individual and national identities, often portraying characters who navigate complex cultural landscapes. For instance, Adichie's *Americanah* addresses the diaspora experience, highlighting how characters grapple with cultural dislocation and the interplay between African and Western identities.

- **Challenges**: While globalization can foster cultural exchange, it also raises concerns about cultural imperialism and the erosion of local traditions. There is an ongoing debate about whether globalization ultimately empowers marginalized voices or exacerbates existing inequalities by privileging dominant cultures. Writers and scholars must navigate these complexities while acknowledging the diverse experiences of globalization.

5.2 Intersectionality in Post-Colonial Discourse

- **Overview**: Intersectionality, a term coined by Kimberlé Crenshaw, emphasizes how various forms of social stratification—such as race, class, gender, and sexuality—intersect to shape individual experiences. In post-colonial contexts, intersectionality provides a nuanced framework for understanding the multifaceted identities of individuals affected by colonial histories.

- **Contemporary Perspective**: Contemporary post-colonial literature increasingly incorporates intersectional analysis, recognizing that the experiences of colonization and its aftermath cannot be reduced to single narratives. Works like *Homegoing* by Yaa Gyasi explore the intersections of race, gender, and historical trauma, illustrating how colonial legacies shape the lives of multiple generations of women.

- **Challenges**: While intersectionality enriches post-colonial studies, it can also complicate analysis. Scholars face the challenge of addressing overlapping identities without reducing individuals to mere categories. There is also the risk of essentialism, where intersectional identities are oversimplified or misrepresented. Careful attention is needed to maintain the complexity of lived experiences.

5.3 Digital Narratives and Technology

- **Overview**: The rise of digital media has transformed storytelling, providing new platforms for post-colonial voices. Social media, blogs, and digital literature enable writers from previously marginalized communities to share their narratives globally, challenging traditional publishing gatekeepers.

- **Contemporary Perspective**: Digital narratives offer innovative ways to engage with post-colonial themes, allowing for real-time commentary on cultural and political issues. Writers like Leila Aboulela and Shailja Patel leverage digital platforms to reach wider audiences, often combining traditional storytelling with modern technology. The use of multimedia in storytelling also allows for more immersive and interactive experiences.

- **Challenges**: Despite the opportunities presented by digital platforms, challenges remain regarding access, representation, and the potential for digital colonialism. Not all voices are equally represented in the digital sphere, and issues of digital divide continue to exist, particularly in regions with limited internet access. Furthermore, the commercialization of digital narratives can dilute the authenticity of post-colonial expressions.

5.4 Environmental Concerns and Eco-Criticism

- **Overview**: As climate change and environmental degradation become increasingly urgent global issues, post-colonial literature is beginning to engage more with ecological themes. Eco-criticism in a post-colonial context examines the impact of colonialism on the environment and how indigenous knowledge systems can offer solutions to contemporary ecological crises.
- **Contemporary Perspective**: Authors like Amitav Ghosh and Arundhati Roy incorporate environmental themes into their narratives, highlighting the interconnectedness of ecological and cultural issues. Ghosh's *The Hungry Tide* illustrates how colonial histories have shaped environmental landscapes, while Roy's *The Ministry of Utmost Happiness* addresses environmental degradation in India.
- **Challenges**: Post-colonial eco-criticism faces challenges in integrating environmental concerns with social justice issues. There is a risk of prioritizing

environmental narratives at the expense of social equity, particularly in communities that are already marginalized. Balancing ecological awareness with the realities of post-colonial struggles requires careful consideration and intersectional analysis.

5.5 Rise of the Global South and Transnationalism

- **Overview**: The concept of the Global South reflects the geopolitical shifts in the world, highlighting the experiences and perspectives of countries historically colonized or marginalized by global powers. Transnationalism emphasizes the interconnectedness of global cultures and the fluidity of identities across borders.
- **Contemporary Perspective**: Post-colonial literature increasingly reflects transnational narratives, where characters navigate multiple national identities and cultural affiliations. Authors like Junot Díaz and Taiye Selasi explore themes of migration and belonging, depicting the complexities of identity in a globalized world.
- **Challenges**: While the focus on the Global South and transnationalism enriches post-colonial discourse, it also raises questions about representation and authenticity. Writers from the Global South may face pressure to conform to Western expectations of "post-colonial" narratives, potentially limiting their artistic freedom. Additionally, the fluidity of identities complicates the notion of a singular "post-colonial" experience.

5.6 The Role of Language in Post-Colonial Literature

- **Overview**: Language plays a crucial role in post-colonial literature, serving as both a medium of expression and a site of struggle. Writers often grapple with the legacy of colonial languages, navigating the tension between using the colonizer's language and reclaiming indigenous languages.
- **Contemporary Perspective**: Many contemporary post-colonial writers, such as Ngũgĩ wa Thiong'o and Zadie Smith, explore the implications of language on identity and cultural expression. Ngũgĩ advocates for writing in indigenous languages as a form of resistance against colonial legacies, while Smith's use of code-switching reflects the multicultural realities of contemporary Britain.
- **Challenges**: The issue of language in post-colonial literature poses challenges related to accessibility and audience reception. Writers who choose to write in Indigenous languages may struggle to reach wider audiences, while those who write in colonial languages risk being critiqued for perpetuating colonial dominance. Balancing linguistic authenticity with the desire for broader communication is a complex task for many writers.

5.7 The Need for Ethical Representation

- **Overview**: As post-colonial literature continues to evolve, the ethical representation of marginalized voices remains a central concern. Scholars and writers grapple with the responsibility of portraying experiences authentically and sensitively.

- **Contemporary Perspective:** The rise of movements advocating for representation and diversity in literature underscores the need for ethical storytelling. Writers are increasingly aware of the power dynamics involved in narrating the experiences of marginalized communities. Collaborations with local voices and indigenous communities have become more common as a means of ensuring authenticity.

- **Challenges:** The challenge lies in balancing authenticity with the complexities of representation. Misrepresentation or oversimplification of experiences can perpetuate stereotypes and harm marginalized communities. Writers must navigate their positionality and ensure that their narratives reflect the richness and diversity of lived experiences without appropriating or exploiting them.

This chapter addresses the contemporary dynamics and challenges facing post-colonial narratives, emphasizing the importance of adapting to a rapidly changing world while maintaining the integrity of the voices and stories emerging from historically marginalized communities. Through examining these perspectives and challenges, the ongoing relevance of post-colonial literature and criticism becomes evident, highlighting the need for continued dialogue and engagement with diverse narratives.

CHAPTER SEVEN

CONCLUSION

The convergence of Indian aesthetic theory and African narratives within this book, *Aesthetic Bridges: Indian Theory Meets African Narratives,* offers profound insights into the intricate web of cultural expressions that illuminate our understanding of beauty, identity, and the human experience. Through the exploration of five core themes—Foundation of Aesthetic Thought, Emotional Landscapes, Performance and Participation, Symbolism and Spirituality, and Post-Colonial Narratives—we have uncovered a rich tapestry of shared meanings and divergent perspectives that reflect the complexities of both traditions.

Our inquiry commenced with a thorough examination of the foundational principles underlying aesthetic thought in Indian and African cultures. We observed how the Indian concept of *rasa*—the emotional flavor experienced by the audience—and the African understanding of art as a communal experience underscore the significance of context in shaping aesthetic appreciation. In Indian aesthetics, theorists like Bharata and Abhinavagupta articulated how emotions are not just personal but collective experiences that resonate with cultural values.

Similarly, in African traditions, art forms are deeply rooted in community, reflecting shared histories and collective identities. By comparing these foundational philosophies, we acknowledge that aesthetics transcends mere beauty; it encapsulates social relations, historical contexts, and cultural narratives. This theme invites us to rethink the definitions of art and aesthetics, moving beyond Western-centric paradigms to appreciate the nuanced ways in which diverse cultures interpret and create beauty. Understanding these foundations is crucial for fostering a more inclusive discourse on aesthetics that recognizes the plurality of human experiences.

The exploration of emotional landscapes has further illustrated the transformative power of art in both traditions. We analyzed how Indian and African narratives engage with a wide array of emotions, reflecting the complexities of human existence. From the deep sorrow expressed in *Joys of Motherhood* by Buchi Emecheta to the ecstatic celebration of love in *The God of Small Things* by Arundhati Roy, emotional depth is a cornerstone for both literary and artistic expressions. Through this theme, we learned that emotions are not universal in their expression but are deeply embedded in cultural contexts. The articulation of grief, joy, love, and resistance in African narratives often intersects with historical trauma and social struggles, while Indian literature frequently explores the intricate dynamics of familial and societal relationships. This comparative analysis underscores how emotional landscapes can serve as sites of resistance and empowerment, revealing the capacity of art to evoke empathy and foster understanding across cultural divides.

The significance of performance and participation in both Indian and African artistic traditions has emerged as a key theme in our discussions. We explored how art is not merely a product to be consumed but an active engagement that invites audiences to participate in the creation of meaning. In Indian classical dance and theater, the *Natya* (performance) is seen as a sacred act, deeply intertwined with spirituality and community. In contrast, African storytelling and rituals often incorporate communal participation, blurring the lines between artist and audience. This theme highlights the importance of understanding art as a dynamic process rather than a static object. The participatory nature of these traditions fosters a sense of belonging and shared identity among community members. By examining the role of performance, we recognize how artistic expressions can catalyze social change and empower marginalized voices, creating spaces for dialogue and resistance.

In our exploration of symbolism and spirituality, we uncovered the profound connections between aesthetic expression and spiritual beliefs in both Indian and African narratives. Symbolism serves as a powerful tool to convey deeper meanings, often rooted in cultural myths, religious practices, and historical contexts. For instance, the use of motifs such as the lotus in Indian art symbolizes purity and spiritual awakening, while African art often incorporates symbols that reflect ancestral ties and cosmological beliefs. Both traditions illustrate how art functions as a medium for spiritual exploration, offering insights into existential questions and the quest for transcendence. This theme emphasizes that aesthetics cannot be divorced from spirituality; rather, they are intertwined in ways that enrich our understanding of both domains. By delving into the symbolic dimensions of art, we appreciate how cultural narratives provide frameworks for individuals to navigate their spiritual journeys and connect with the cosmos.

Finally, the theme of post-colonial narratives has illuminated how both Indian and African writers grapple with the legacies of colonialism and the quest for identity in a globalized world. We examined how these narratives challenge dominant discourses, reclaim cultural identities, and articulate the complexities of post-colonial existence. In the works of authors such as Chimamanda Ngozi Adichie and Salman Rushdie, we see how the intersections of race, gender, and history complicate notions of belonging and identity. Post-colonial literature serves as a site for resistance against neocolonial narratives and offers platforms for marginalized voices to be heard. This exploration of post-colonialism underscores the importance of understanding how historical injustices continue to shape contemporary realities, urging us to engage critically with the ongoing effects of colonialism in both Indian and African contexts.

In conclusion, *"Aesthetic Bridges: Indian Theory Meets African Narratives"* invites readers to embrace the richness of cultural exchange and the diverse aesthetic expressions that emerge from it. The themes explored throughout this book reveal that aesthetics is a deeply relational and context-dependent phenomenon that transcends geographical boundaries. As we navigate an increasingly interconnected world, it becomes vital to recognize and celebrate the aesthetic bridges that connect us. By appreciating the shared human experiences reflected in art and literature, we can foster empathy, understanding, and solidarity across cultures. This book serves as a call to engage with the complexities of aesthetic thought and to honor the diverse narratives that enrich our collective human heritage. Ultimately, the journey of exploring aesthetic bridges is not merely an academic endeavor but a celebration of the profound connections that unite us as human beings. It is an invitation to continue questioning, learning, and appreciating the intricate web of narratives that shape our understanding of beauty, identity, and the human experience. Through this exploration, we aspire to cultivate a world that honors the richness of its cultural tapestries, recognizing that our differences are not barriers but bridges to deeper understanding and connection.

References

References

1. Achebe, Chinua. *Things Fall Apart*. London: Heinemann, 1958.
2. Achebe, Chinua. *Morning Yet on Creation Day: Essays.* Anchor Books, 1975.
3. Adichie, Chimamanda Ngozi. *Half of a Yellow Sun.* London: Fourth Estate, 2006.
4. Aidoo, Ama Ata. *The Dilemma of a Ghost.* London: Longman, 1965.
5. Aidoo, Ama Ata. *Changes: A Love Story*. New York: The Feminist Press, 1991.
6. Anandavardhana. *Dhvanyaloka*. Translation by Daniel H. H. Ingalls. Cambridge: Harvard University Press, 1990.
7. Anzaldúa, Gloria. *Borderlands/La Frontera: The New Mestiza.* Aunt Lute Books, 1987.
8. Appiah, Kwame Anthony. *In My Father's House: Africa in the Philosophy of Culture.* Oxford University Press, 1992.
9. Appadurai, Arjun, et al. *The Social Life of Things: Commodities in Cultural Perspective.* Cambridge University Press, 1986. (Discusses the role of objects and symbols in performance across cultures).
10. Ashcroft, Bill, Gareth Griffiths, and Helen Tiffin. *The Empire Writes Back: Theory and Practice in Post-Colonial Literatures.* Routledge, 1989.
11. Bhabha, Homi K. *The Location of Culture.* Routledge, 1994.
12. Bâ, Mariama. *So Long a Letter.* Translated by Modupe Bode-Thomas. London: Heinemann, 1981.
13. Bhamaha. *Kavyalankara*. Edited by V. Raghavan. Delhi:

Motilal Banarsidass, 1970.

14. Bhattacharya, V. S. *The Rasa Theory in Shaping Indian Aesthetics*. Motilal Banarsidass Publishers, 2002.

15. Bharata Muni. *NātyaShastra*. Translation by Manmohan Ghosh. Calcutta: The Royal Asiatic Society of Bengal, 1951.

16. Bharucha, Rustom. *Theatre and the World: Performance and the Politics of Culture*. Routledge, 1990.

17. Coomaraswamy, Ananda K. *The Dance of Shiva: Fourteen Indian Essays*. New York: Noonday Press, 1957.

18. Chari, V. K. *Sanskrit Criticism and Theory of Literature*. University of Hawaii Press, 1990.

19. Clifford, James. *Routes: Travel and Translation in the Late Twentieth Century*. Harvard University Press, 1997.

20. Dharwadker, Aparna. *Theatres of Independence: Drama, Theory, and Urban Performance in India Since 1947*. University of Iowa Press, 2005.

21. Emecheta, Buchi. *Second Class Citizen*. London: Heinemann, 1974.

22. Emecheta, Buchi. *The Joys of Motherhood*. London: Heinemann, 1979.

23. Finnegan, Ruth. *Oral Literature in Africa*. Open Book Publishers, 2012.

24. Gates Jr., Henry Louis, and Nellie Y. McKay, editors. *The Norton Anthology of African American Literature*. Norton, 1997.

25. Idowu, E. Bolaji. *African Traditional Religion: A Definition*. SCM Press, 1973.

26. Kapferer, Bruce. *A Celebration of Demons: Exorcism and the Aesthetics of Healing in Sri Lanka*. Indiana University Press, 1991.

27. Kuntaka. *Vakroktijivita*. Edited by K. Krishnamoorthy.

Dharwar: Karnataka University Press, 1977.

28. Mbiti, John S. *African Religions and Philosophy.* Heinemann, 1969.

29. Ngugi wa Thiong'o. *Decolonising the Mind: The Politics of Language in African Literature.* Heinemann, 1986.

30. Nketia, J. H. Kwabena. *African Music in Ghana: A Review of Forms and Techniques.* Evanston: Northwestern University Press, 1963.

31. Nketia, J. H. Kwabena. *The Music of Africa.* W. W. Norton & Company, 1974.

32. Nyambi, Oliver. "Memory, Emotion, and Subjectivity in African Narratives." *Journal of African Cultural Studies,* vol. 33, no. 1, 2021, pp. 33-49.

33. Raghavan, V. *Some Concepts of Alankara Shastra.* Madras: Adyar Library, 1978.

34. Ramanujan, A. K. *The Collected Essays of A. K. Ramanujan.* Oxford University Press, 1999.

35. Said, Edward. *Orientalism.* Pantheon Books, 1978.

36. Said, Edward. *Culture and Imperialism.* Knopf, 1993.

37. Samuelson, Meg. "Affective Geographies and Emotions in African Postcolonial Literature." *Research in African Literatures,* vol. 40, no. 2, 2009, pp. 31-47.

38. Schechner, Richard. *Performance Theory.* Routledge, 2003.

39. Shulman, David. *More Than Real: A History of the Imagination in South India.* Harvard University Press, 2012.

40. Vatsyayan, Kapila. *Classical Indian Dance in Literature and the Arts.* New Delhi: Sangeet Natak Akademi, 1968.

41. Okpewho, Isidore. *African Oral Literature: Backgrounds, Character, and Continuity.* Bloomington: Indiana University Press, 1992.